ART BOOKS

FROM CRESCENT MOON PUBLISHING

Leonardo da Vinci
by James Pearson

Early Netherlandish Painting
by Rosalind Mutter

Piero della Francesca
by Naomi Haskell

Giovanni Bellini
by Julia Davis

Eric Gill: Nuptials of God
by Anthony Hoyland

Minimal Art and Artists In the 1960s and After
by Laura Garrard

Postwar Art
by George Knighton

Vincent van Gogh: Visionary Landscapes
by Stuart Morris

Max Beckmann
by Stuart Morris

Egon Schiele: Sex and Death in Purple Stockings
by D. Simon Eade

Mark Rothko: The Art of Transcendence
by Julia Davis

Jasper Johns
by L.M. Poole

Brice Marden
by Laura Garrard

Frank Stella: American Abstract Artist
by James Pearson

FRAGONARD

FRAGONARD

BY HALDANE MACFALL

CRESCENT MOON

First published 1909. This edition © 2020.

Set in Book Antiqua 10 on 14pt.
Designed by Radiance Graphics.

British Library Cataloguing in Publication data

ISBN-13 9781861716415

CRESCENT MOON PUBLISHING
P.O. Box 1312, Maidstone, Kent, ME14 5XU
Great Britain, www.crmoon.com

CONTENTS

NOTE ON THE TEXT

The text is from *Fragonard* by Haldane MacFall, and published by Frederick A. Stokes Company, New York, 1909/ 1912.

The illustrations in the original text are included in the illustrations section, along with many other works.

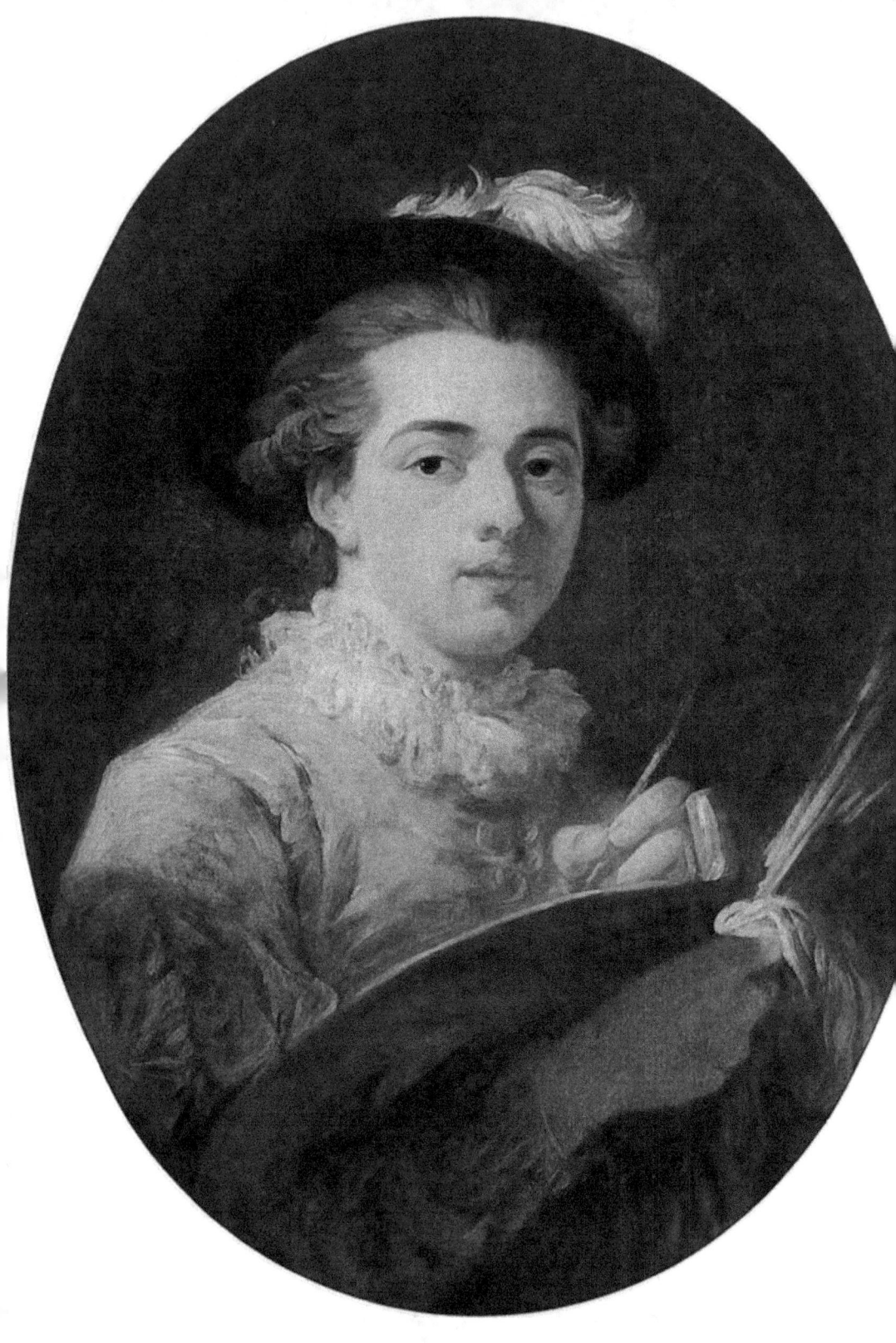

Jean Honoré Fragonard, Self-Portrait, 1760-70

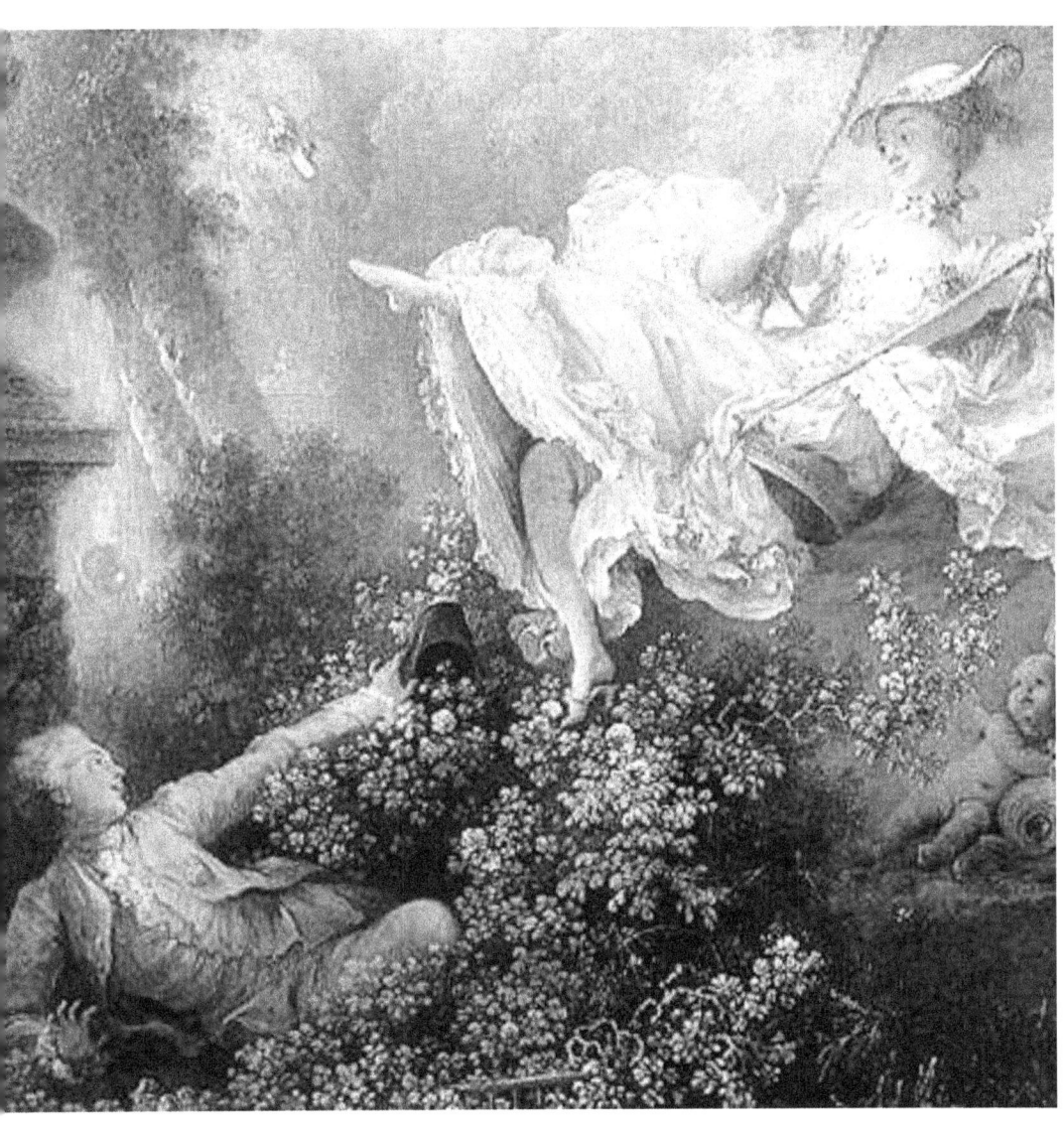

Jean Honoré Fragonard, The Swing, 1767, detail

TO

MY FRIEND

WALTER EMANUEL

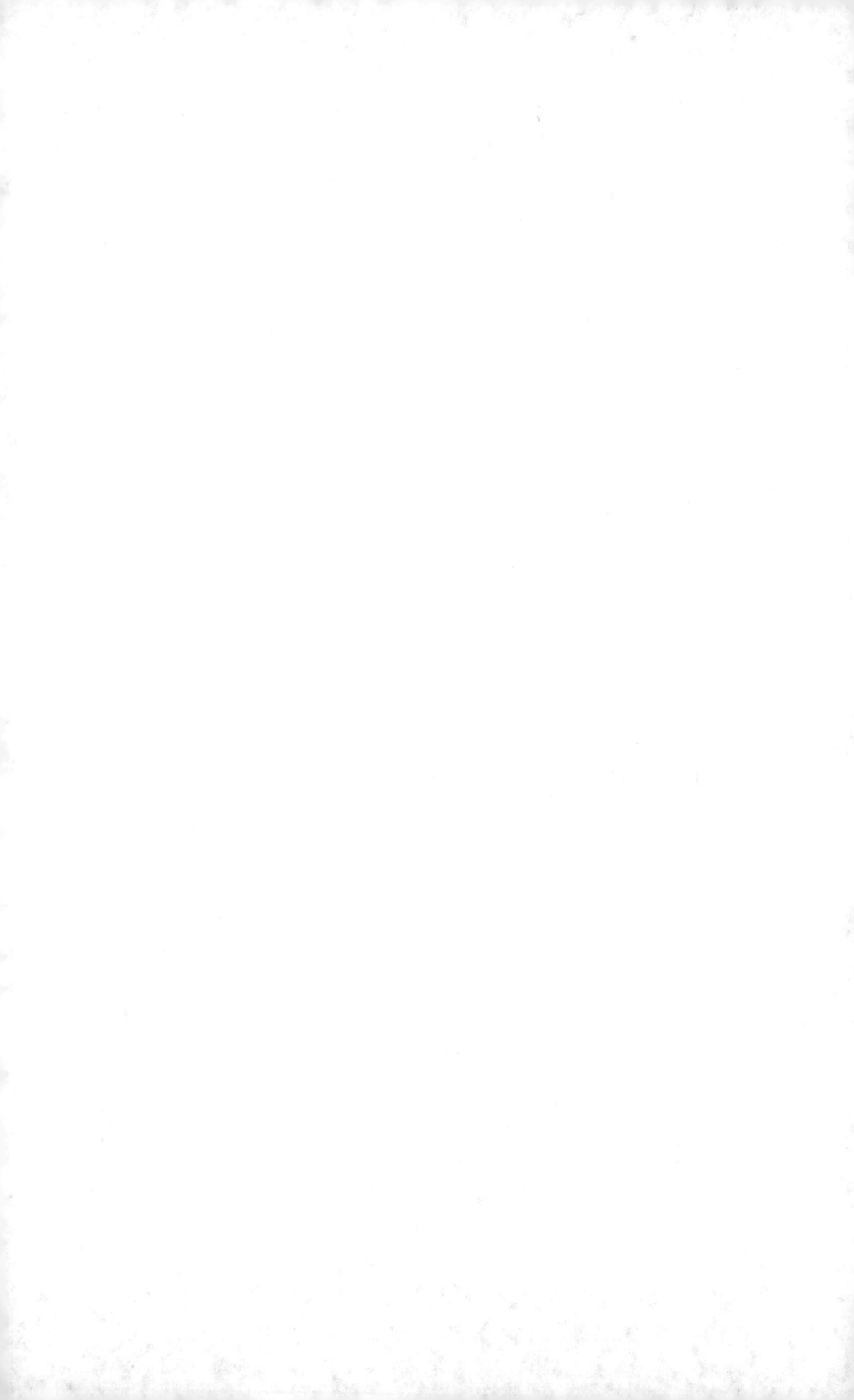

I

THE BEGINNINGS

High up, amongst the Sea-Alps that stretch along the southern edge of France, where romantic Provence bathes her sunburnt feet in the blue waters of the Mediterranean, high on the mountain's side hangs the steep little town of Grasse, embowered midst grey-green olive-trees. In as sombre a narrow street as there is in all her dark alleys, on the fifth day of April in the much bewigged and powdered year of 1732, there was born to a glovemaker of the town, worthy mercer Fragonard, a boy-child, whom the priest in the gloomy church christened Jean Honoré Fragonard.

As the glovemaker looked out of his sombre house over the sunlit slopes of the grey-green olive-trees that stretched away to the deep blue waters of the sea, he vowed his child to commerce and a thrifty life in this far-away country place that was but little vexed with the high ambitions of distant, fickle, laughing Paris, or her splendid scandals; nay, scarce gave serious thought to her gadding fashions or her feverish vogues – indeed, the attenuated ghosts of these once frantic things wriggled southwards through the provinces on but sluggish feet to the high promenades of Grasse – as the worthy mercer was first in all the little town to know by his modest traffic in them; and that, too, only long after the things they shadowed were buried under new millineries and fopperies and fantastic riot in the gay capital. As a fact, the dark-eyed, long-nosed folk that trudged these steep and narrow thoroughfares were a sluggish people; and sunlit Grasse snored away its day in drowsy fashion.

But if the room where the child first saw the light were gloomy enough within, the skies were wondrous blue without, and the violet-scented slopes were robed in a tender garment of silvery green, decked with the gold of orange-trees, and enriched with bright embroidery of many-coloured flowers that were gay as the gayest ribbons of distant Paris. And the glory of it bathed the lad's eyes and heart for sixteen years, so that his hands got them itching to create the splendour of it which sang within him; and the wizardry of the flower-garden of France never left him, casting its spell over all his thinking, and calling to him to utter it to the world. It stole into his colour-box, and on to his palette, and so across the canvas into his master-work, and was to lead him through the years to a blithe immortality.

The small boy with the big head was born in the year after François Boucher came back to Paris from his Italian wanderings on the eve of his thirties and won to academic honour. The child grew up in his Provençal home, whilst Boucher, turning his back upon academic art on gaining his seat at the Academy, was creating the Pastorals, Venus-pieces, and Cupid-pieces that changed the whole style of French art from the pompous and mock-heroic manner of Louis Quatorze's century of the sixteen hundreds to the gay and elegant pleasaunces that fitted so aptly the elegant pleasure-seeking days of Louis the Fifteenth's seventeen hundreds.

Gossip of high politics came trickling down to Grasse as slowly as the fashions, yet the eleven-year-old boy's ears heard of the death of the minister, old Cardinal Fleury, and of the effort of Louis to become king by act. Though Louis had small genius for the mighty business, and fell thenceforth into the habit of ruling

France from behind petticoats, raising the youngest of the daughters of the historic and noble house of De Nesle to be his accepted consort under the rank and honours of Duchess of Chateauroux. All tongues tattled of the business, the very soldiery singing mocking songs; when – Louis strutting it as conqueror with the army, got the small-pox at Metz, and sent the Chateauroux packing at the threat of death. He recovered, to enter Paris soon after as the Well-Beloved, and to be reconciled with the frail Chateauroux before she died in the sudden agony in which she swore she had been poisoned.

At thirteen the boy listened to the vague rumours of a new scandal that set folk's tongues wagging again throughout all France. The king raised Madame Lenormant d'Etioles, a daughter of the rich financier class, to be Marquise de Pompadour, and yielded up to her the sceptre over his people.

The nations, weary of war, agreed to sign the Peace of Aix-la-Chapelle in 1748. In this, our artist's sixteenth year, the Pompadour had been the king's acknowledged mistress for three years. From this time, the peace being signed, Louis the Fifteenth laid aside all effort to fulfil the duties of the lord over a great people; gave himself up to shameless and riotous living, and allowed the Pompadour to usurp the splendour of his throne and to rule over the land.

For the next sixteen years she was the most powerful person at court, the greatest personality in the State – making and unmaking ministers like a sovereign, and disposing of high offices, honours, titles, and pensions. The king squandered upon her some seventy odd millions of the public money as money is now valued. Her energy and her industry must have been colossal. Her intelligence saved the king from the boredom of decision in difficult affairs. She made herself a necessity to his freedom from care. Every affair of State was discussed and settled under her guidance. Ministers, ambassadors, generals, transacted their business in her handsome boudoirs. She dispensed the whole patronage of the sovereign with her pretty hands. The prizes of the army, of the church, of the magistracy, could only be secured through her good-will. As though these things were not load enough to bow the shoulders of any one human being she kept a rein upon every national activity. She created the porcelain factory of Sèvres, thereby adding a lucrative industry to France. She founded the great military school of Saint Cyr. She mothered every industry. She was possessed of a rare combination of talents and accomplishments, and of astounding taste. But her deepest affection was for the arts.

The Pompadour had gathered about her, as the beautiful Madame d'Etioles, the supreme wits and artists and thinkers of her day; Voltaire and Boucher and Latour and the rest were her friends, and the new thought that was being born in France was nursed in her drawing-rooms. As the Pompadour she kept up her friendships. She was prodigal in her encouragement of the arts, in the furnishment of her own and the king's palaces and castles. And it was in the exercise and indulgence of her better qualities that she brought out the genius and encouraged to fullest achievement the art of Boucher, and of the great painters of her time. So Boucher brought to its full blossom the art that Watteau had created – the picture of "Fêtes galentès" – and added to the artistic achievement of France the Pastorals wherein Dresden shepherds and shepherdesses dally in pleasant landscapes, and the Venus-pieces wherein Cupids flutter and romp – a world of elegance and charm presided over by the Goddess of Love.

II

ROME

All this was but Paris-gossip amidst the olive-trees and steep streets of far-away Grasse, where the large-headed, small-bodied lad was idling through his fifteen summers, living and breathing the beauty of the pleasant land of romance that bred him, when, like bolt from the blue, fell the news upon him that his father, tearing aside the fabric of the lad's dreams, had articled him as junior clerk to a notary.

But the French middle-class ideal of respectability meant no heaven for this youth's goal, no ultimate aim for his ambition. He idled his master into despair; "wasting his time" on paint-pots and pencil-scribblings until that honest man himself advised that the lad should be allowed to follow his bent.

So it came about – 'twas in that year of the Treaty of Aix-la-Chapelle, the year that saw the Pompadour come to supreme power (she had been for three years the king's acknowledged mistress) – the youth's mother, with all a French mother's shrewdness and common-sense, gathered together the sixteen-year-old lad's sketches, and bundled off with him in a diligence to Paris.

Arrived in Paris she sought out the greatest painter of the day, and burst with the shy youth into the studio of the dandified favourite artist of the king's majesty, Pompadour's Boucher – large-hearted, generous, much-sinning, world-famed Boucher, then at the very summit of his career – he was at that time living in the Rue Grenelle-Saint-Honoré, which he was about to leave, and in which Fragonard in his old age was destined to end his days.

The lad glanced with wonder, we may be sure, at the great "Rape of Europa" that stood upon the master's easel, whilst his mother poured out in the rough accent of Provence the tale of the genius of her son – stole, too, a stealthy scrutiny of the Venus-pieces and Pastorals that stood about the studio, and was filled with awed admiration. The mother besought the genius of France to make a genius of her son; and Boucher, with kindly smile upon his lips, glancing over the immature work of the prodigy, told the lad that he might come back to him in six months' time, pointing out to him, with all that large-hearted friendliness and sympathy that made him the loved idol of the art-students, that he lacked sufficient dexterity in the use of his tools to enter his studio or to benefit by apprenticeship to him, and advising the anxious mother to take him to Chardin as the supreme master in France from whom to learn the mastery of his craft.

To Chardin the youth went; and France's consummate master in the painting of still-life, putting the palette on the youngster's thumb straightway, from the very first day – as his custom was – and making him use sienna upon it as his only pigment, advising him as he went, set him to the copying of the prints from the masterpieces of his own time, insisting on his painting large and broad and solid and true.

Young Fragonard made so little progress that Chardin wrote to his parents that he could get nothing out of him; and sent the lad, bag and baggage, out of his studio.

Thrown upon his own resources, the young fellow haunted the churches of Paris, brooded over the masterpieces that hung therein, fixed them in his mind's eye, and, returning to his lodging, painted them, day by day, from memory.

At the end of six months he called again upon Boucher, his sketches under his arm; and this time he was not sent away. Astounded at the youth's progress, struck by his enthusiasm, Boucher took him into his studio, and set him to work to prepare the large decorative cartoons that artists had to make from their paintings for use at the Gobelins and Beauvais looms. The artist painted his picture "in little"; he was also required to paint an "enlargement" of the size that the weavers had to make into tapestry – this enlargement was mostly done by pupils, the State demanding, however, that the artist should work over it sufficiently to sign his name upon it – the head of the factory keeping custody of the "painting in little" to guide him; the weavers working from the enlargement. This work upon the enlargement of Boucher's paintings was an ideal training for Fragonard.

The Director-General of Buildings to the king (or, as we should nowadays call him, Minister of Fine Arts), Lenormant de Tournehem, kinsman to the Pompadour, died suddenly in the November of 1751; the Pompadour promptly caused to be appointed in his place her brother Abel Poisson de Vandières – a shy, handsome youth, a gentleman, a man of honour, who brought to his office an exquisite taste, a loyal nature, and marked abilities. The king, who liked him well, and called him "little brother," soon afterwards created him Marquis de Marigny – and Fragonard, like many another artist of his day, was to be beholden to him.

After a couple of years' training under Boucher, Fragonard's master, with that keen interest that he ever took in the efforts and welfare of youth, and particularly of his own pupils, urged the young fellow to compete for the Prix de Rome, pointing out to him the advantages of winning it. At twenty, without preparation, and without being a pupil of the Academy, Fragonard won the coveted prize with his "Jeroboam Sacrificing to Idols." It was in this year that Boucher was given a studio and apartments at the Louvre.

For three years thereafter, Fragonard was in the king's school of six *élèves protégés* under Carle Van Loo. He continued to work in Boucher's studio, as well as painting on his own account; and it is to these years that belong his "Blind Man's Buff" and several pictures in this style.

Meanwhile the quarrels between priests and parliaments had grown very bitter. The king took first one side, then the other. It was in 1756, Louis having got foul of his Parliament, that the unfortunate and foolish Damiens stabbed the king with a penknife slightly under the fifth rib of his left side, as he was stepping into his carriage at Versailles, and suffered by consequence the terrible tortures and horrible death that were meted out to such as attempted the part of regicide.

This was the year when, at twenty-four, Fragonard was entitled to go to Rome at the king's expense – the Italian tour being a necessary part of an artist's training who desired to reach to academic distinction, and honours in his calling. He started on his journey to Italy with Boucher's now famous farewell advice ringing in his ears: "My dear Frago, you go into Italy to see the works of Raphael and Michael Angelo; but – I tell you in confidence, as a friend – if you take those fellows seriously you are lost." ("Lost" was not the exact phrase, Boucher being a Rabelaisian wag, but it will pass.)

Arrived in Rome, Fragonard, like his master before him, was torn with doubts and uncertainties and warring influences. For several months he did no work, or little work; and though he stood before the masterpieces of Michael Angelo and Raphael, stirred by the grandeur of their design, and eager to be busy with his brush, he was too much of a Frenchman, too much in sympathy with the French genius, too much enamoured of the art of his master, to be affected creatively by them. His hesitations saved him, and won France a master in her long roll of fame. He escaped the taint of learning to see through the eyes of others, evaded the swamping of his own genius in an endeavour to utter his art in halting Italian. Rome was not his grave, as it has been the grave of so many promising young sons of France; and he came out of the danger a strong and healthy man. Tiepolo brought him back vision and inspiration, and the solid earth of his own age to walk upon. And the French utterance of his master Boucher called back his dazed wits to the accents of France. At last the genius that was in him quickened and strove to utter itself.

The bright colours of Italy, the glamour of her landscapes, these were the living lessons that bit deeper into his art than all the works of her antique masters; and the effort to set them upon his canvas gave to his hand's skill an ordered grace and dignity that were of more vital effect upon his achievement than the paintings of the great dead.

So it came about that Natoire, then director of the royal school in the Villa Mancini, having written his distress to Marigny at the young fellow's beginnings, was soon writing enthusiastically about him, and procured a lengthening of his stay in Rome.

Here began that lifelong friendship with Hubert Robert, already making his mark as an artist, and with the Abbé de Saint-Non, a charming character, who was to engrave the work of the two young painters, and greatly spread their names abroad thereby. Saint-Non's influential relations procured him free residence in the Villa d'Este, where the other two joined him, and a delightful good-fellowship between the three men followed – the Abbé's artistic tastes adding to the bond of comradeship. So two years passed pleasantly along at the Villa d'Este, one of the most beautiful places in all Italy – the ancient ruins hard by, and the running waters and majestic trees leaving an impression upon Fragonard's imagination, which passed to his canvases, and never left his art – developing a profound sense of style, and a knowledge of light and air that bathed the scenes he was to paint with such rare skill and insight. Here grew that love of stately gardens which are the essence of his landscapes, and which won to the heart of a child of Provence.

In distant Paris the making of history was growing apace. Gossip of it reached to Italy. A backstairs intrigue almost dislodged the Pompadour from power. D'Argenson and the queen's party threw the beautiful and youthful Madame de Choiseul-Romanet, not wholly unflattered at the adventure, into the king's way to lure him from the favourite. The king wrote her a letter of invitation. The girl consulted her noble kinsman, the Comte de Stainville, of the Maurepas faction or queen's party, a bitter enemy to the Pompadour. De Stainville, his pride of race wounded that a kinswoman of his should be offered to the king, went to the Pompadour, exposed the plot, and forthwith became her ally – soon her guide in affairs of State.

In the midst of disasters by sea and land the Pompadour persuaded the king to send for De Stainville, and to make him his Prime Minister. He was created Duc de Choiseul in December 1758. He had as ally one of the most astute and subtle and daring minds in eighteenth-century France – his sister Beatrice, the famous Duchesse de Grammont. The king found a born leader of men. Choiseul brought back dignity to the throne. He came near to saving France. Choiseul was the public opinion of the nation. He founded his strength on Parliament and on the new philosophy. He became a national hero. He could do no wrong. He rose to power in 1758; and at once stemmed the tide of disaster to France.

The Parliament men took courage. Philosophy, with one of its men in power, spoke out with no uncertain voice. All France was listening.

Fragonard had at last to turn his face homewards; and dawdling through Italy with Saint-Non, staying his feet at Bologna and Venice awhile, the two friends worked slowly towards Paris, Fragonard entering his beloved city, after five wander-years, in the autumn of 1761, in his twenty-ninth year, untainted and unspoiled by academic training, his art founded upon that of Boucher, enhanced by his keen study of nature. He reached Paris, rich in plans for pictures, filled with ardour and enthusiasm for his art, ambitious to create masterpieces, and burning to distinguish himself.

III

THE DU BARRY

When Fragonard came back to Paris on the edge of his thirtieth year it was to find that a great change had come over his master Boucher. The old, light-hearted, genial painter was showing signs of the burning of the candle of life at both ends. His art also was being bitterly assailed by the new critics – the new philosophy was asking for ennobling sentiments from the painted canvas, and the teaching of a moral lesson from all the arts. Boucher stood frankly bewildered, blinking questioning eyes at the frantic din. Old age had come upon him, creeping over the shrewd kindly features, dulling the exquisite sight. He could not wholly ignore the change that was taking place in public taste. The ideas of the philosophers were penetrating public opinion. The man of feeling had arisen and walked in the land. They were beginning to speak of the great antique days of Greece and Rome. Fickle fashion was about to turn her back upon Dresden shepherds and shepherdesses and leafy groves, and to take up her abode awhile with heroes and amongst picturesque ruins.

Arrived in Paris, Fragonard at once set himself to the task of painting the historic or mythologic Academy-piece expected from the holder of the Prix de Rome on return from the Italian tour. He painted "The High Priest Coresus slaying himself to save Callirhoë," which, though badly hung at the Salon, and still to be seen at the Louvre, was hailed with high praise by the academicians and critics. The only adverse criticisms of coldness and timidity levelled against it sound strange in the light of his after-career, which, whatever its weaknesses, was not exactly marked with coldness nor eke with timidity.

For two years thereafter he essayed the academic style.

But the praises of Diderot and Grimm failed to fill his pockets; and he decided to paint no more academic pieces for the critics' praise. He had indeed no taste for such things, no sympathy with ancient thought nor with the dead past. He was, like his master, a very son of France – a child of his own age, glorying in the love of life and the beauty of his native land.

Having done his duty by his school, he turned his back upon it gleefully, as Boucher had also done before him, and set himself joyously to the painting of the life about him.

His great chance soon came, and in strange guise.

It so happened that a young blood at the court, one Baron de Saint-Julien, went to the painter Doyen with his flame, and asked him to paint a picture of the pretty creature being swung by a bishop whilst he himself watched the display of pretty ankles as the girl went flying through the air. Doyen had scruples; but recommended Fragonard for the naughty business.

Fragonard seized the idea readily enough, except that he made the frail girl's husband swing the beauty for her lover's eyes, using the incident, as usual, but as the trivial theme for a splendid setting amidst trees, glorying in the painting of the foliage – as you may see, if you step into the Wallace galleries, where is the exquisite thing that brought Fragonard fame – the world-famous "Les hazards heureux de l'Escarpolette."

The effect was prodigious. De Launay's brilliant engraving of it popularised it throughout the land. Nobles and rich financiers, and all the gay world of fashion besides, now strove to possess canvases signed by Fragonard. Boucher was grown old and ailing; and just as Boucher had been the painter of the France of fashion under the Pompadour, so Fragonard was now to become the mirror of the court, of the theatre, of the drawing-room, of the boudoir, of the age of Du Barry.

Finding a ready market for subjects of gallantry, he gave rein to his natural bent, and straightway leaped into the vogue. Pictures were the hobby of the nobility and the rich; and France under the Pompadour, and particularly at this the end of her reign, was madly spendthrift upon its hobbies and fickle fancies. The pretty house, delicately tinted rooms, fine furniture, dainty decorations, and charming pictures, were a necessity for such as would be in the fashion.

You shall look in vain for the affected innocence, the naïve mawkishness, the chaste sentimentality of Greuze in the master-work of Fragonard. He knew nothing of these things – cared less. His was an ardent brush; and he used it ardently; but always you shall find him using his subject, however naughty, as the mere excuse for a glorious picture of trees. He is one of the great landscape-painters of France.

He had many qualities that go to make a decorative painter. Indeed, it is to the Frenchmen of the seventeen-hundreds to whom we may safely go for pictures that make the walls of a drawing-room a delight. Unlike the Italians, they are pleasing to live with. His painting of "La Fête de St. Cloud," in the dining-room of the Governor of the Bank of France, is one of the decorative landscapes of the world.

He was now producing works in considerable numbers – it is his first, his detailed period, somewhat severe in arrangement and style as to composition and handling – the years of "Love the Conqueror," the "Bolt," the "Fountain of Love," of "Le Serment d'Amour," the "Gimblette," "Les Baigneuses," the "Sleeping Bacchante," the "Début du modèle," and the like.

His master, Boucher, was grown old; he could not carry out the commissions for the decoration of rooms and for paintings with which he was overwhelmed; and it was in order to help forward his brilliant pupil, his "Frago," that he now introduced him to his old friend and patron the farmer-general Bergeret de Grandcour – a man of great wealth, a lover of art, and an honorary member of the Royal Academy – who became one of Fragonard's most lavish patrons and most intimate friends. Bergeret de Grandcour commissioned several panels in this, Fragonard's thirty-fifth year – the year of his painting the superb "Fête de St. Cloud." This is towards the end of that period of minute and detailed painting which he did with such consummate skill, yet without bringing pettiness into his largeness of conception.

Meantime, Choiseul's masterly mind, having secured peace abroad, saw that France, if she were to keep her sovereign State, must be first cleansed from the dangers that threatened from within. He turned to the blotting out of the turbulent order of the Jesuits, whose vindictive acts against, and quarrels with, the Parliaments, and whose galling and oppressive tyranny, had roused the bitter hatred of the magistracy and of the people throughout the land. Choiseul they treated as their bitterest enemy. He decided to blot them out, root and branch, from France. The popular party closed up its ranks. Choiseul had not long to wait. The chance came in odd fashion enough. An attempt by the Order to end the Pompadour's scandalous relations with the king was the quaint thing – the match that started the explosion. With all his skill of state-craft, Choiseul leaped to the weapon. In secret concert with the king's powerful favourite he struck at them through the bankruptcy of their banking concerns in the West Indies, caused by their losses in the wars with England; and Louis abolished the society out of the land, secularising its members, and seizing its property.

The Pompadour lived but a short while to enjoy her triumph. Worn-out by her vast activities, and assailed by debt, she fell ill of a cough that racked her shrunken body. She died, transacting the king's business and affairs of State, on the 15th of April 1764, in her forty-second year.

Whatever may be said of this cold-blooded, calculating,

grasping woman, who crushed down every nice instinct of womanhood to win a king's favour, who knew no scruple, who was without mercy, without pardon or forgiveness, without remorse; bitter and adamant in revenge; who turned a deaf ear to the cries from the Bastille; whose heart knew no love but for self; it must be allowed that at least for Art she did great and splendid service. She not only encouraged and brought out the best achievement of her age; she did Art an even more handsome benefit. She insisted on artists painting their age and not aping the dead past.

To Fragonard personally she rendered no particular service. His real achievement began on the eve of her death, when she was a worn-out and broken woman. Nor had Fragonard ever that close touch with the royal house or its favourites during any part of his lifetime that meant so much to the fortunes of his master, Boucher.

There were two patrons for whom Fragonard was about to create a series of masterpieces in the decoration of their splendid and luxurious homes – works of Art which were to have strange adventures and histories. They were both women.

For the prodigal and eccentric dancer, the notorious Mademoiselle Guimard, he undertook the painting of a series of panels. The Guimard was the rage of Paris – she of the orgic suppers and the naughty dances with her comrade Vestris. Frago, who is said to have been more than a friend of the reckless one of the nimble feet, undertook the decoration of her house in the Chaussée d'Antin, known to the bloods as the Temple of Terpsichore. He painted for the same room a portrait of the frail beauty as an opera-shepherdess – the simple pastoral life was the pose of this unsimple age. He was engaged upon the business, off and on, for several years; and the many delays at last fretted the light one. Fragonard, anything but energetic, liked always to take his own time at his work. The Guimard got to pestering him – she had a sharp tongue – and at last, one fine day, upbraided him roundly, taunting him with a sneer that he would never get the work finished. Fragonard lost patience and temper, goaded by her ill-manners, her abuse, and her biting tongue. "It *is* finished," said he; and walked out of the house. The Guimard could never get him back; but one day he slipped in alone, painted the set dancer's-smile from the dancer's mouth, and placed there instead a snarl upon her lips.

Before this breach between them Fragonard had painted several portraits of the Guimard.

However, the work for the lady was to have far-reaching results little dreamed of. For the completion of the room, Fragonard procured the commission for David, then twenty-five; and David never forgot the service rendered. He was to repay it tenfold when black days threatened; and with rare courage, when even the courage of gratitude was a deadly dangerous commodity.

However, this was not as yet; the sun shone in the skies; and all was gaiety and laughter still.

The "Chiffre d'Amour," the picture of a pretty girl who cuts her lover's monogram in the bark of a tree's trunk, the shadowed tree and figure telling darkly against the glamorous half light beyond, was one of Fragonard's happiest inspirations of these years, as any one may see who steps into the Wallace galleries. Here also may be seen to-day the exquisite "Fair-haired Boy." The boldly painted "L'Heure de Berger" was wet upon the canvas about this year, though its boldness of handling foretells his later manner, whilst the spirit of Boucher is over all.

Four years after the death of the Pompadour the patient neglected queen, amiable dull Marie Leczinska, followed her supplanter to the grave. The king's grief and contrition and his solemn vows to mend his ways came somewhat over-late; they lasted little longer than the drying of his floods of tears over the body of his dead consort.

On the Eve of Candlemas, the first day of February 1769, at a convivial party in Paris that was not wholly without political significance, a Jesuit priest raised his glass *To the Presentation!*

adding after the toast – "To that which has taken place to-day, or will take place to-morrow, the presentation of the new Esther, who is to replace Haman and release the Jewish nation from oppression!"

He spoke figuratively – it was safer so. But 'twas understood. Indeed, the pretty sentiment was well received by the old aristocrats and young bloods about the table; and they drank a bumper to the pretty Madame du Barry. For the Jesuits had no love for the king's minister Choiseul – and the madcap girl was but the lure whereby the king was to be drawn from his great minister. So religion rallied about the frail beauty, and hid behind her extravagant skirts – one of which cost close on £2000 – and, with the old nobility, drank damnation to the king's minister and To the devil with the new thought and with parliaments. Long live the king and the divine right of kings!

Our worthy priest seems to have had the ear of destiny, though he dated his certainty near upon a couple of months too soon.

So it came about that before a year was out the old king was become the doting creature of a light-o'-love of Paris, the transfigured milliner and street-pedlar, Jeanne, natural child of one Anne Béqus, a low woman of Vaucouleurs. This Jeanne, of no surname and unknown father, a pretty, kindly, vulgar child of the gutters, with fair hair and of madcap habits, was some twenty-six years of age, when – being reborn under a forged birth-certificate at the king's ordering, as Anne de Vaubernier, and being married by the same orders to the Count du Barry, an obliging nobleman of the court – she appeared at Versailles as the immortally frail Countess du Barry.

The remonstrances of Choiseul with the king against this new degradation of the throne of France, and his unconcealed scorn and disgust of the upstart countess, made a dangerous enemy for France's great minister, and was to cost him and his France very dear.

The king's infatuation brought royalty into utter contempt

amongst the people. It was to cost France a terrible price – and Fragonard not least of all.

One of the first gifts from the king to the Du Barry was the little castle of Louveciennes; and she proceeded with reckless extravagance to furnish her handsome home. Drouais, the artist, sold to her for 1200 livres (double florins), as overdoors for one of the rooms, four panels that he had bought from Fragonard. They have vanished; but they served Fragonard a good turn – he received an order to decorate Du Barry's luxurious pavilion of Luciennes, which she had had built to entertain the king at her "little suppers."

Thus it chanced that for this wilful light-o'-love Fragonard painted the great master-work of his life – the five world-famous canvases of the series of "The Progress of Love in the Heart of Maidenhood," or, as they are better known, "The Romance of Love and Youth" – the old king masquerading therein as a young shepherd, and the Du Barry as a shepherdess. In "The Ladder" ("L'Escalade" or "Le Rendezvous") the Du Barry plays the part of a timid young girl who starts as she sees her shepherd-lover to be the king; the "Pursuit" follows; then the "Souvenirs" and "Love Crowned." The last of the five, the discarded mistress in "Deserted," was only begun; and was not completed by Fragonard until twenty years later at Grasse, to complete the set.

What it was that struck a chill into the frail Du Barry's favour, so that the masterpieces of Fragonard never entered within her doors, is not fully known. Whatsoever the cause, these canvases were rejected by her. It is said that the work was found to be disappointing, being lacking as to the indecencies by the Du Barry and the king, who preferred the more suggestive panels of Vien. It is true that Fragonard's earlier four panels which she possessed were in questionable taste, and that these five were pure; indeed, their trivial story matters little amidst the massy foliage and the majestic trees that spring into the swinging heavens. Fragonard suspected, and somewhat resented the suspicion, that he was being made to paint in a sort of artistic duel with Vien. At any rate, Vien was chosen. So it came that the discarded pictures lay in Fragonard's studio for over twenty years, when we shall see them, rolled up, making a chief part of the strange baggage of Fragonard's flight from his beloved Paris.

The fact was that the Du Barry was of the gutter. She had the crude love of fineries of the girl promoted from the gutter. She loved display. But into her home she brought the vulgar singers of the lowest theatres, where the Pompadour had brought the wits and leading artists of her time. The old culture was gone. Louis laughed now at ribald songs, and was entertained by clowns.

It is part of the irony of life that Fragonard, who never entered into the favourite's friendship, should have become the recognised artist of her day. It was a part of that grim irony that caused the Du Barry, whose age he honours, to reject the most exquisite work of his hands – in which his art is seen at its highest achievement, the tender half-melancholy of the thing stated with a lyric beauty that displays his genius in its supreme flight.

A search through the Du Barry's bills – and there are four huge bound volumes of them – reveals the list of pictures painted by Boucher, by Vien, by Greuze, and by others, for the spendthrift woman; but of transaction with Fragonard there is no slightest hint.

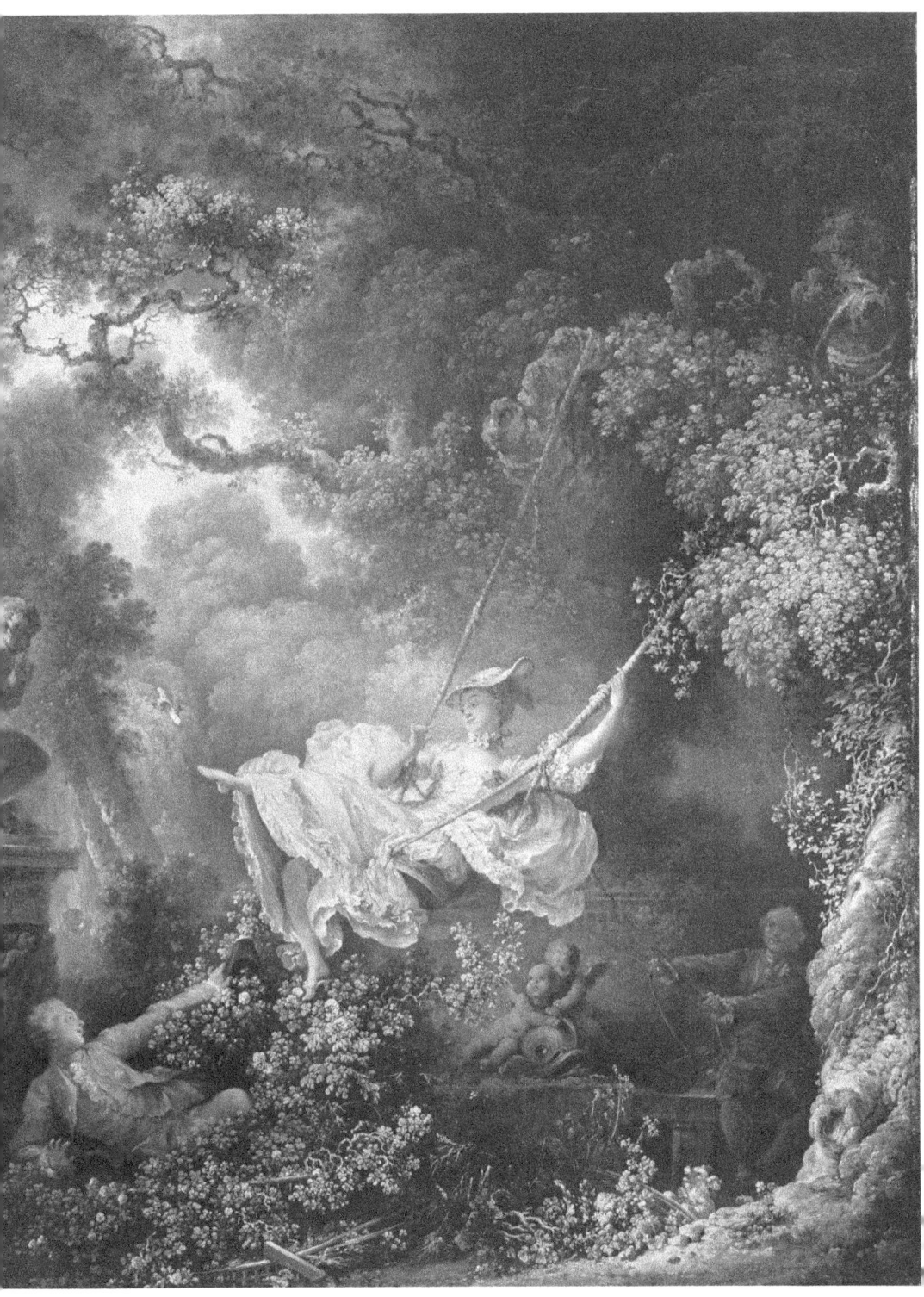

Jean Honoré Fragonard, The Swing, 1767

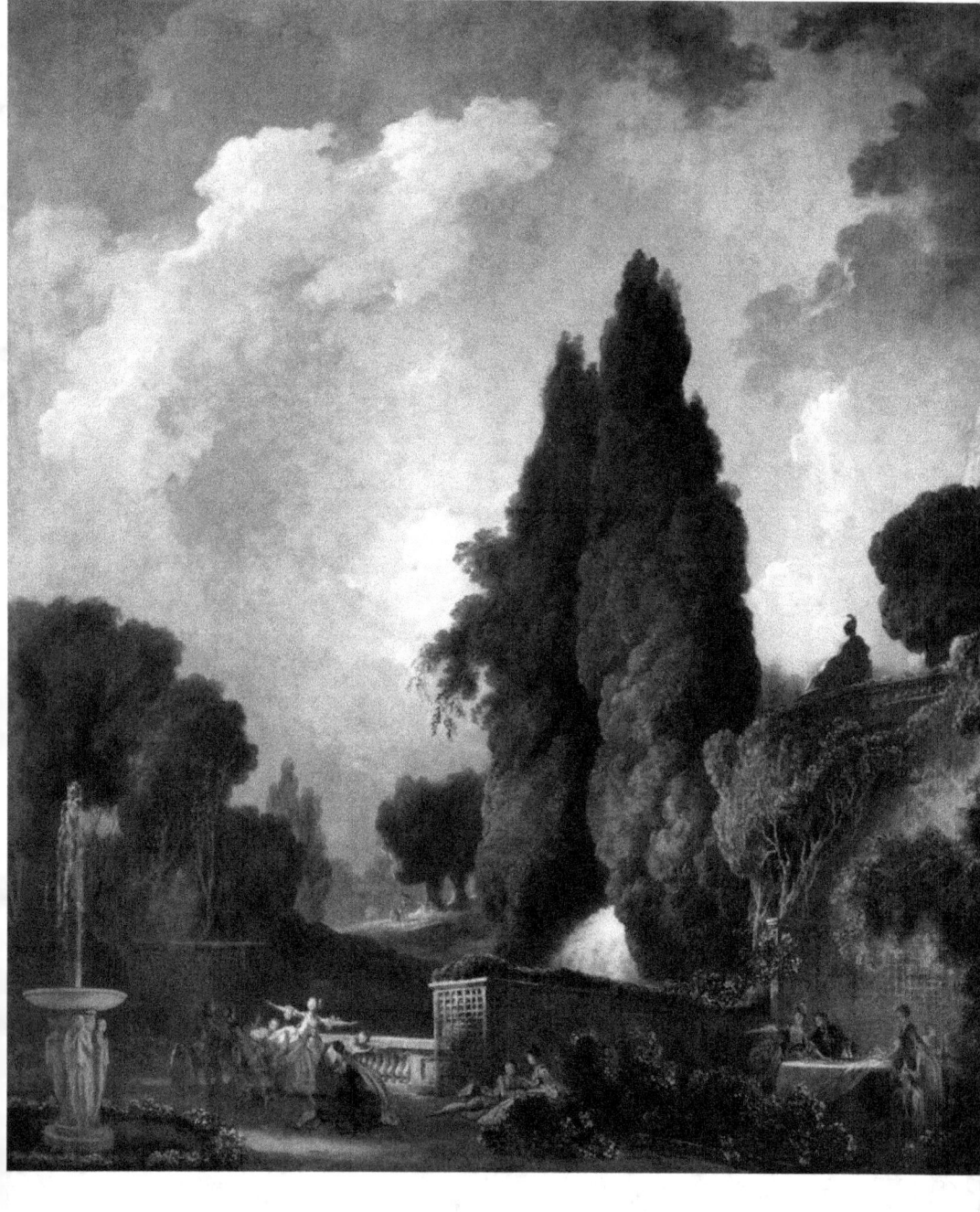

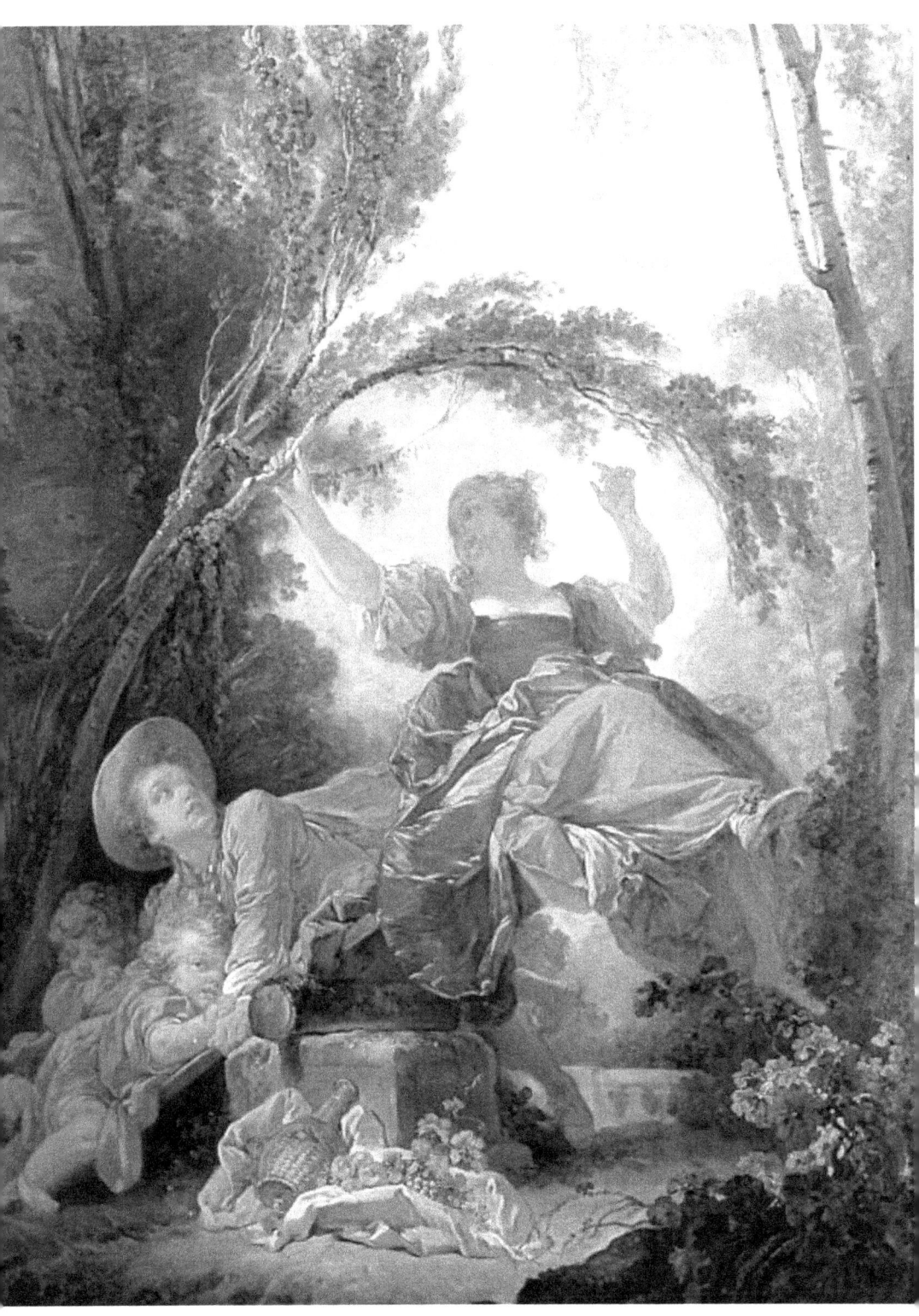

Jean Honoré Fragonard, The See Saw, 1750-75

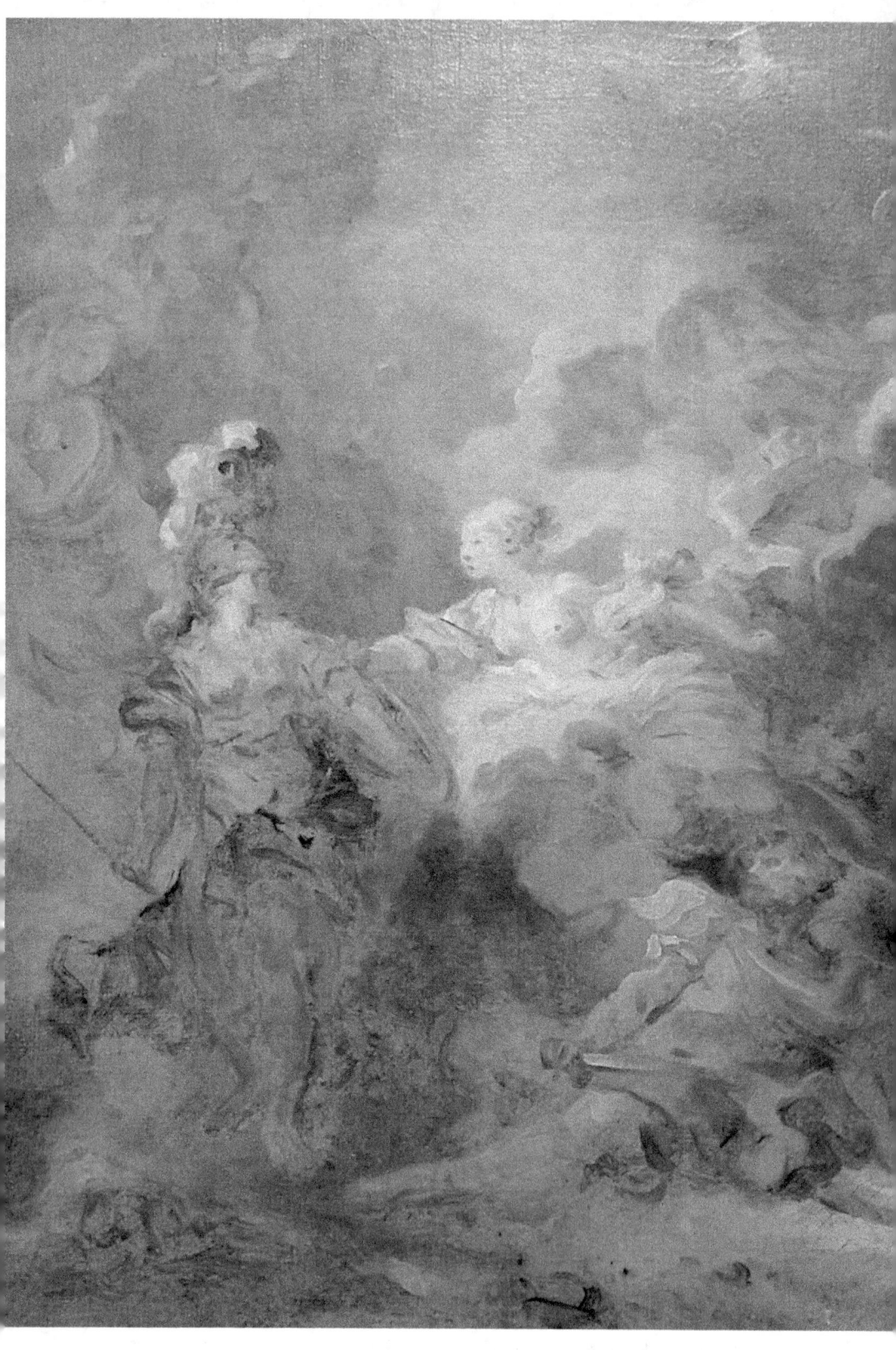

Jean Honoré Fragonard, Le Combat de Minerve contre Mars

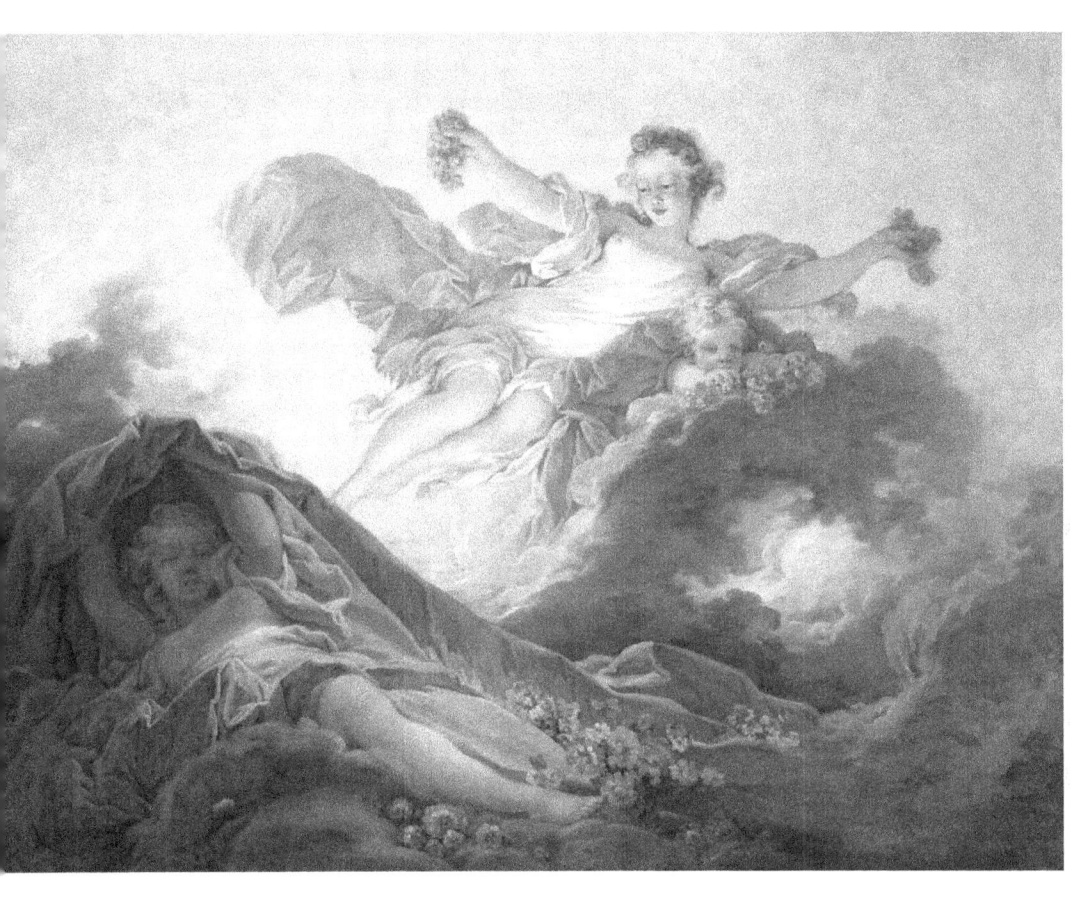

Jean Honoré Fragonard, Aurora, 1775-76

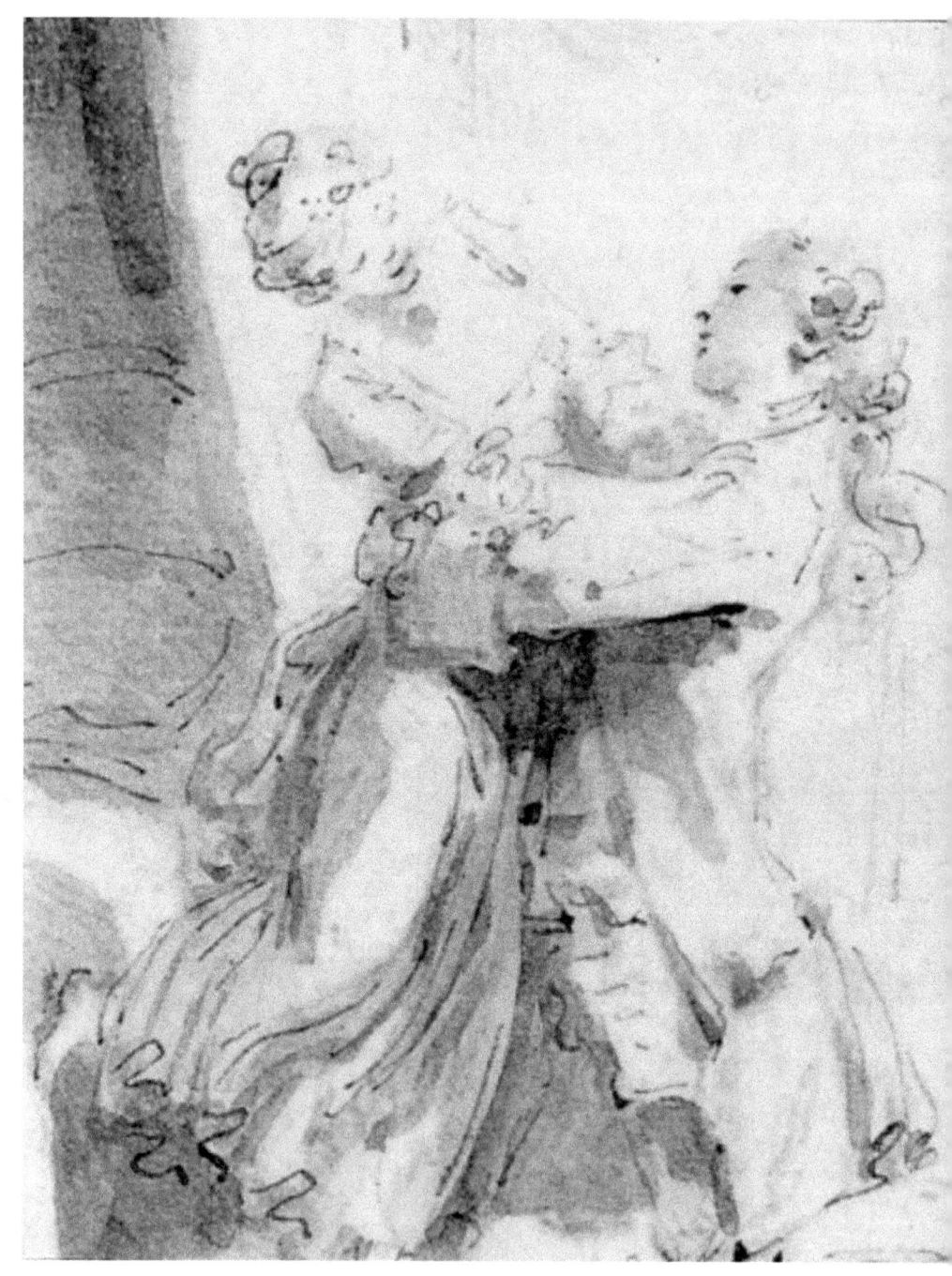

Jean Honoré Fragonard, Libertines, 1770

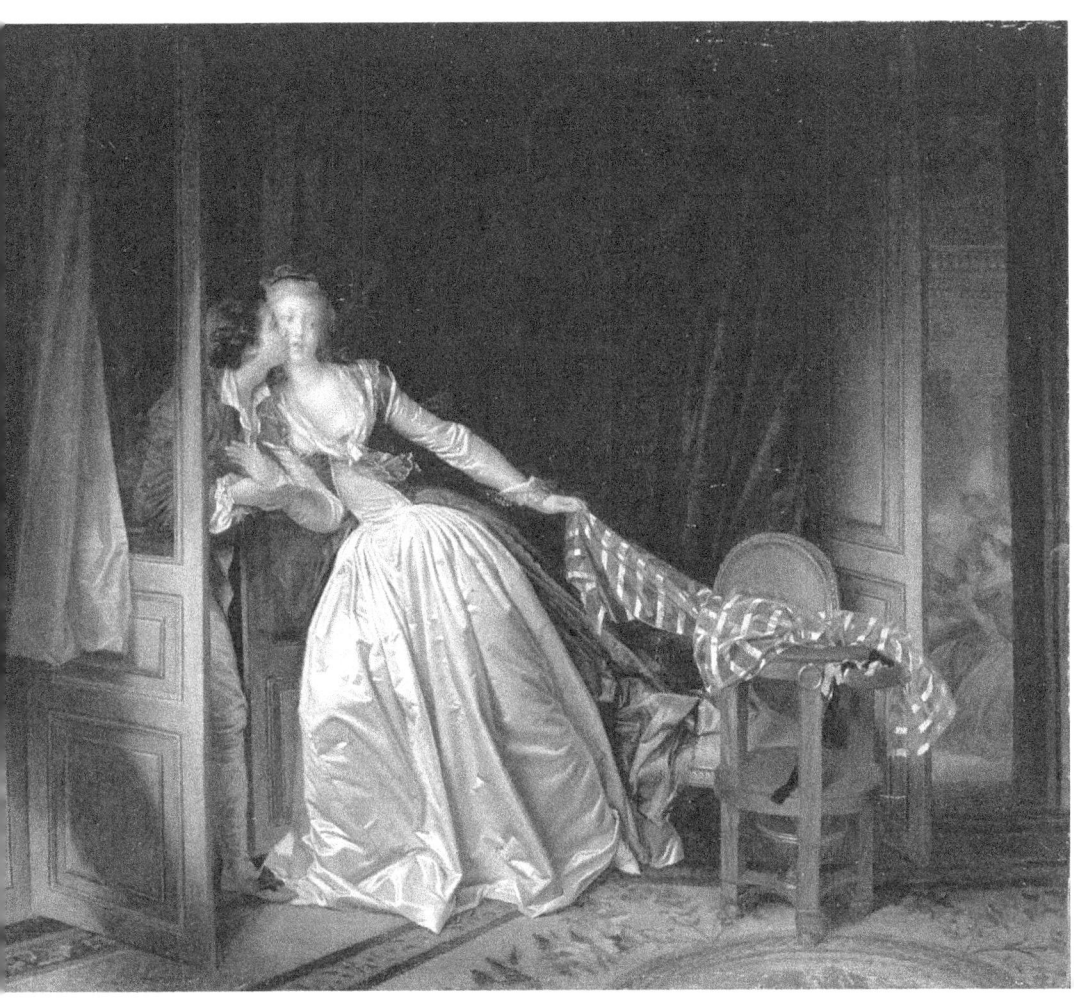

Jean Honoré Fragonard, The Stolen Kiss, late 1780s

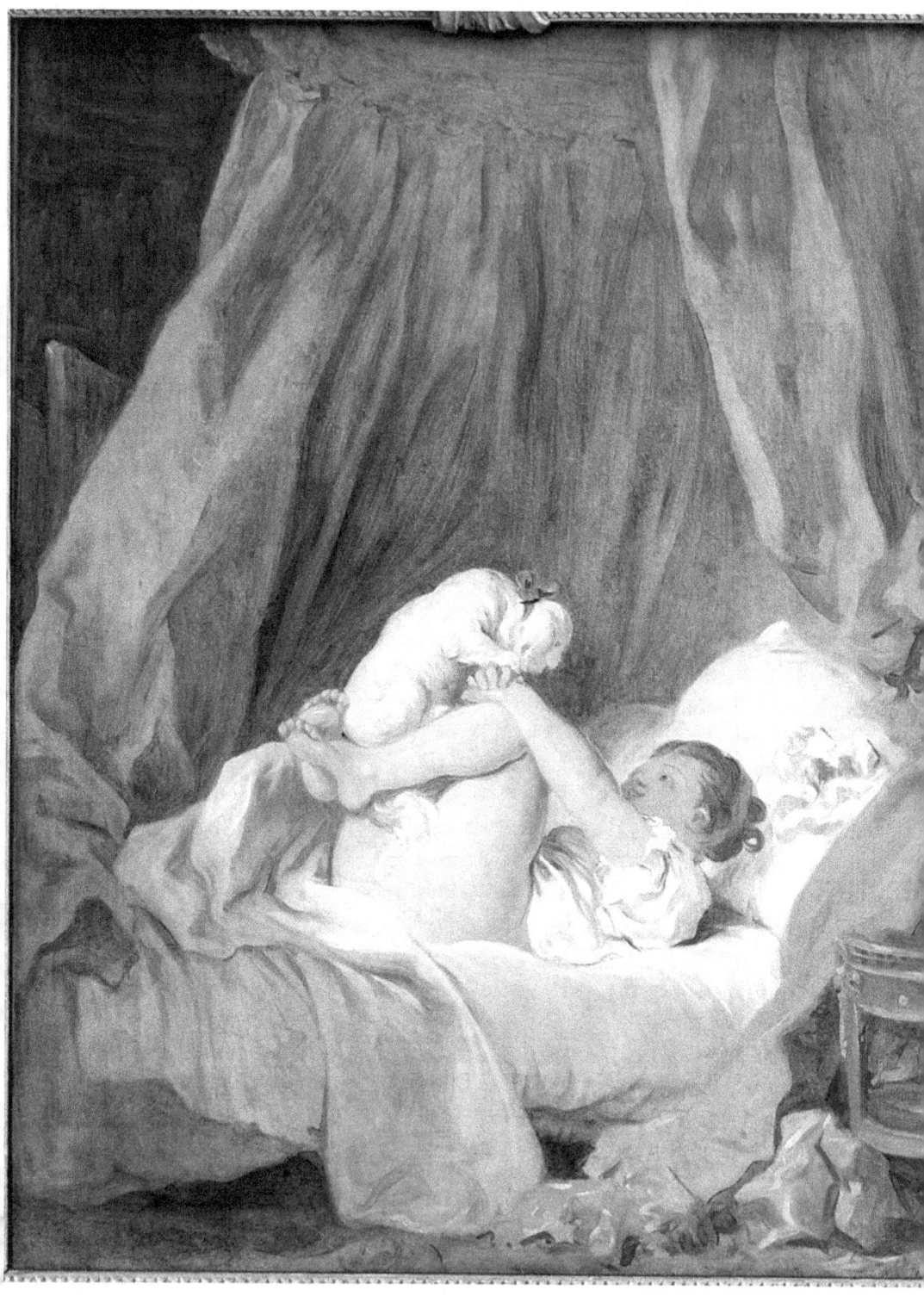

Jean Honoré Fragonard, Jeune Fille et son chien, 1770-75, Alte Pinakothek, Munich

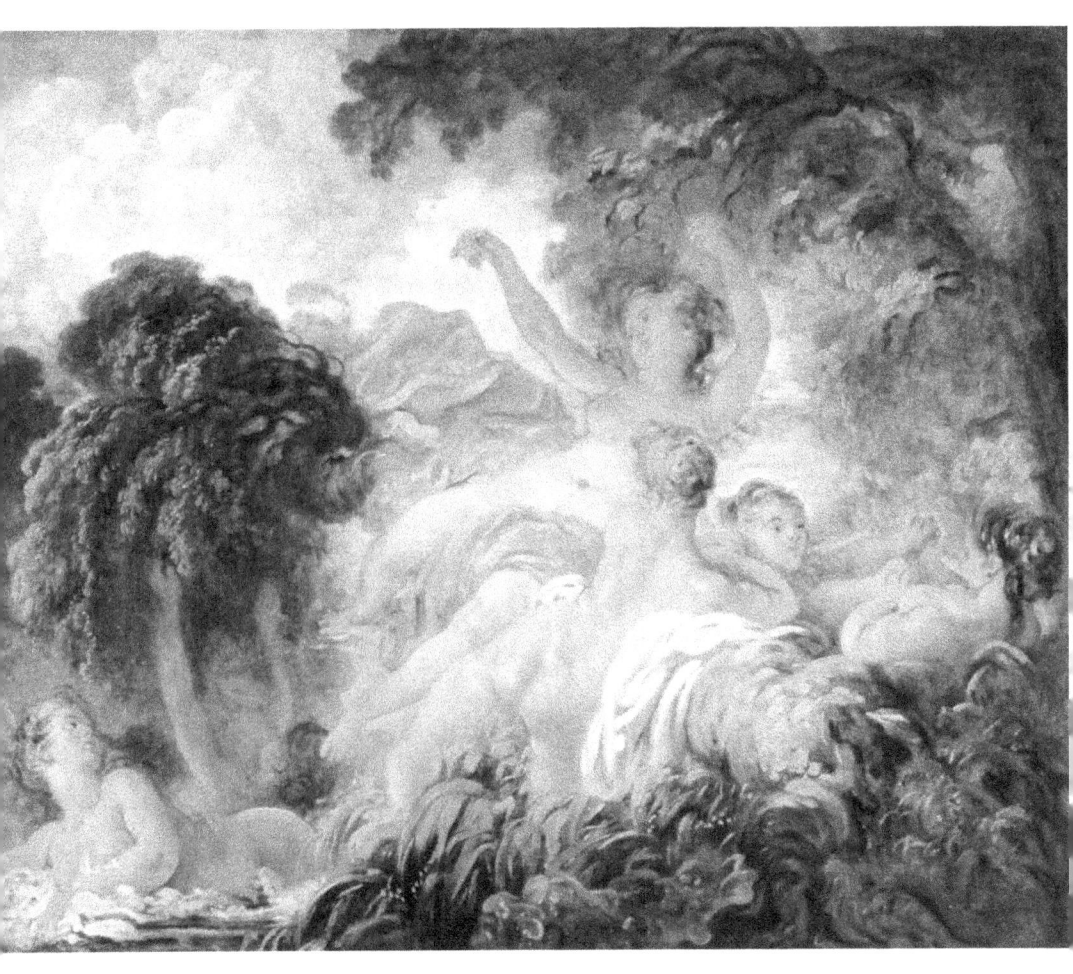

Jean Honoré Fragonard, Bathers, 1756

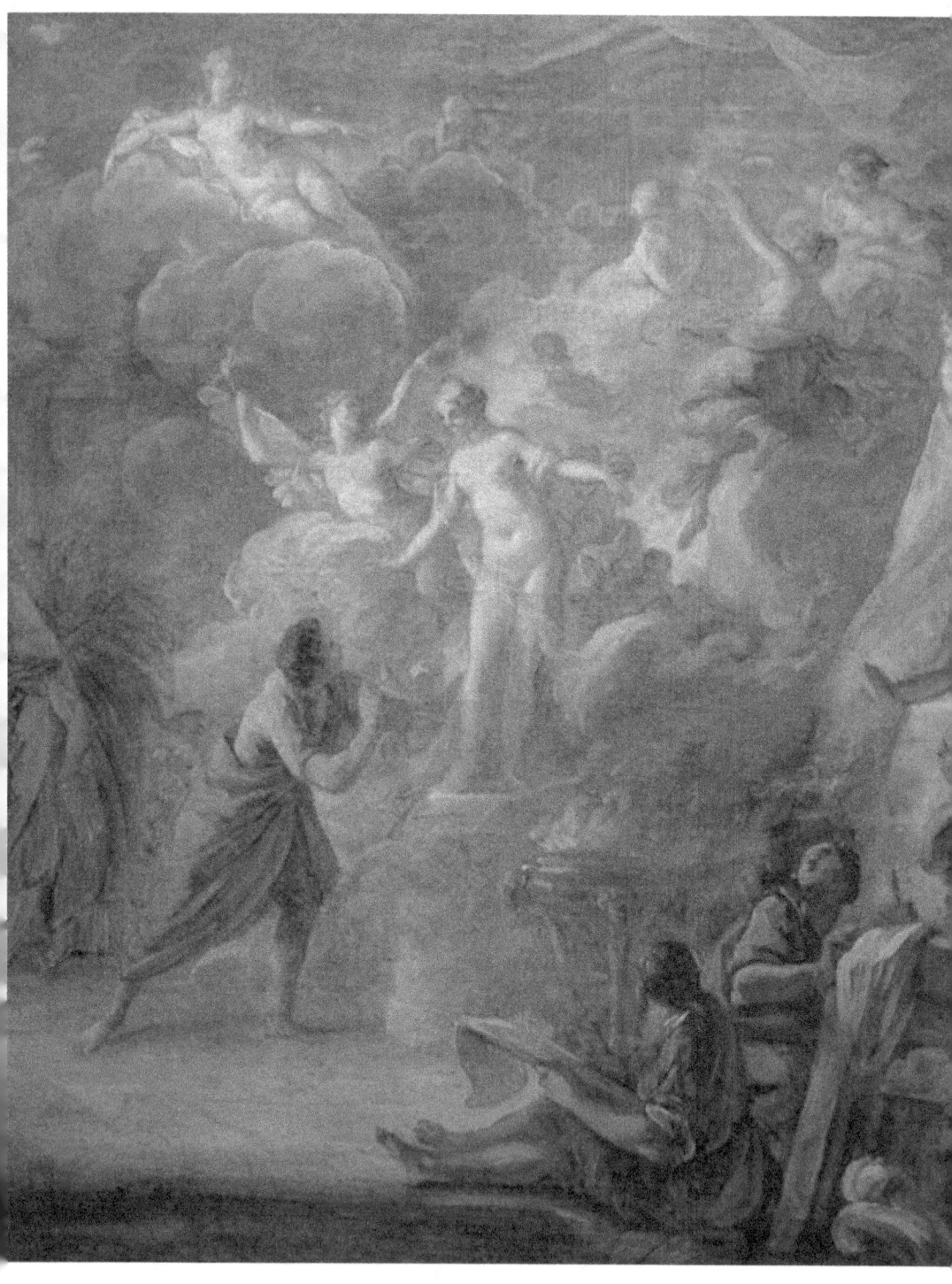

Jean Honoré Fragonard, Pygmalion, Bourges

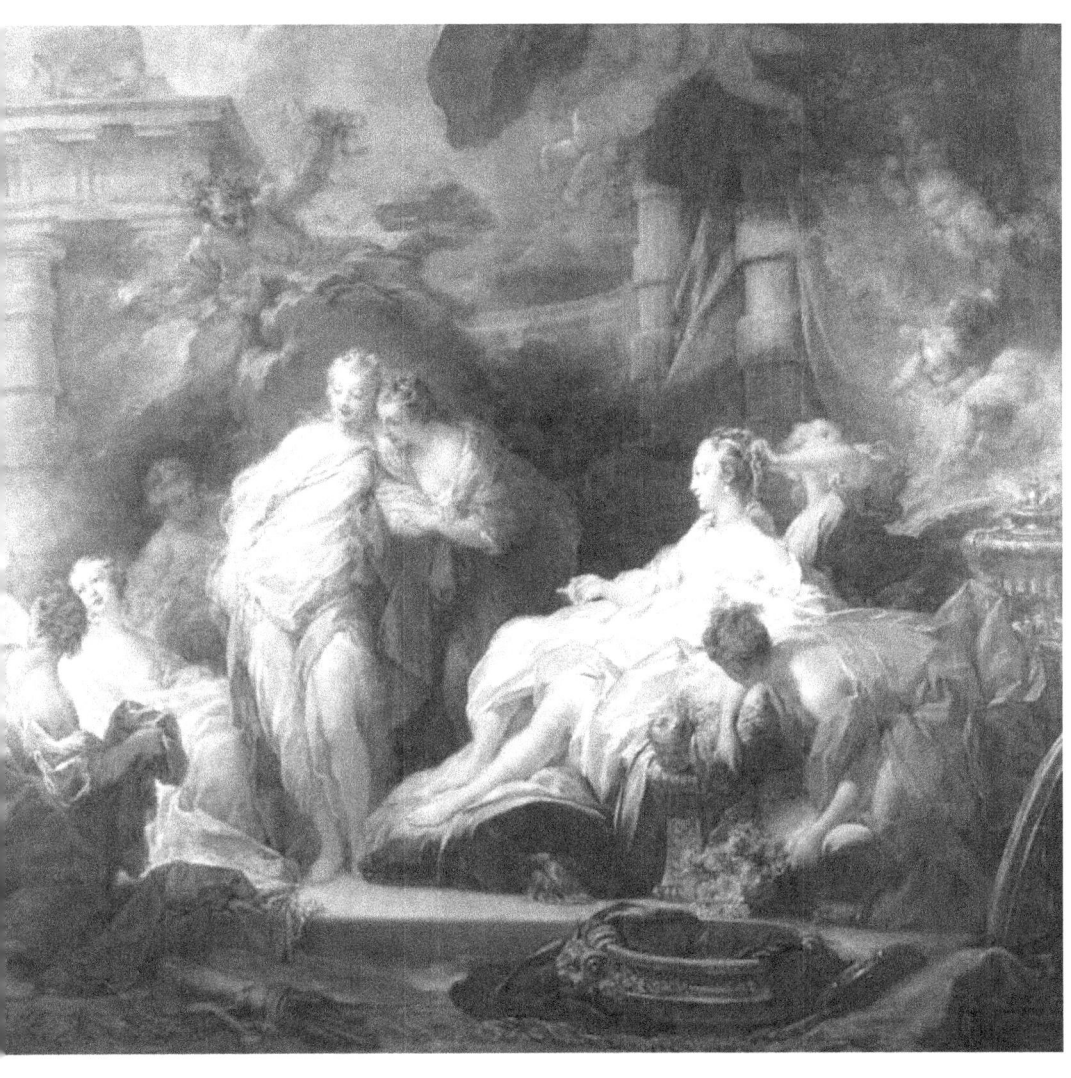

Jean Honoré Fragonard, Psyche, 1753

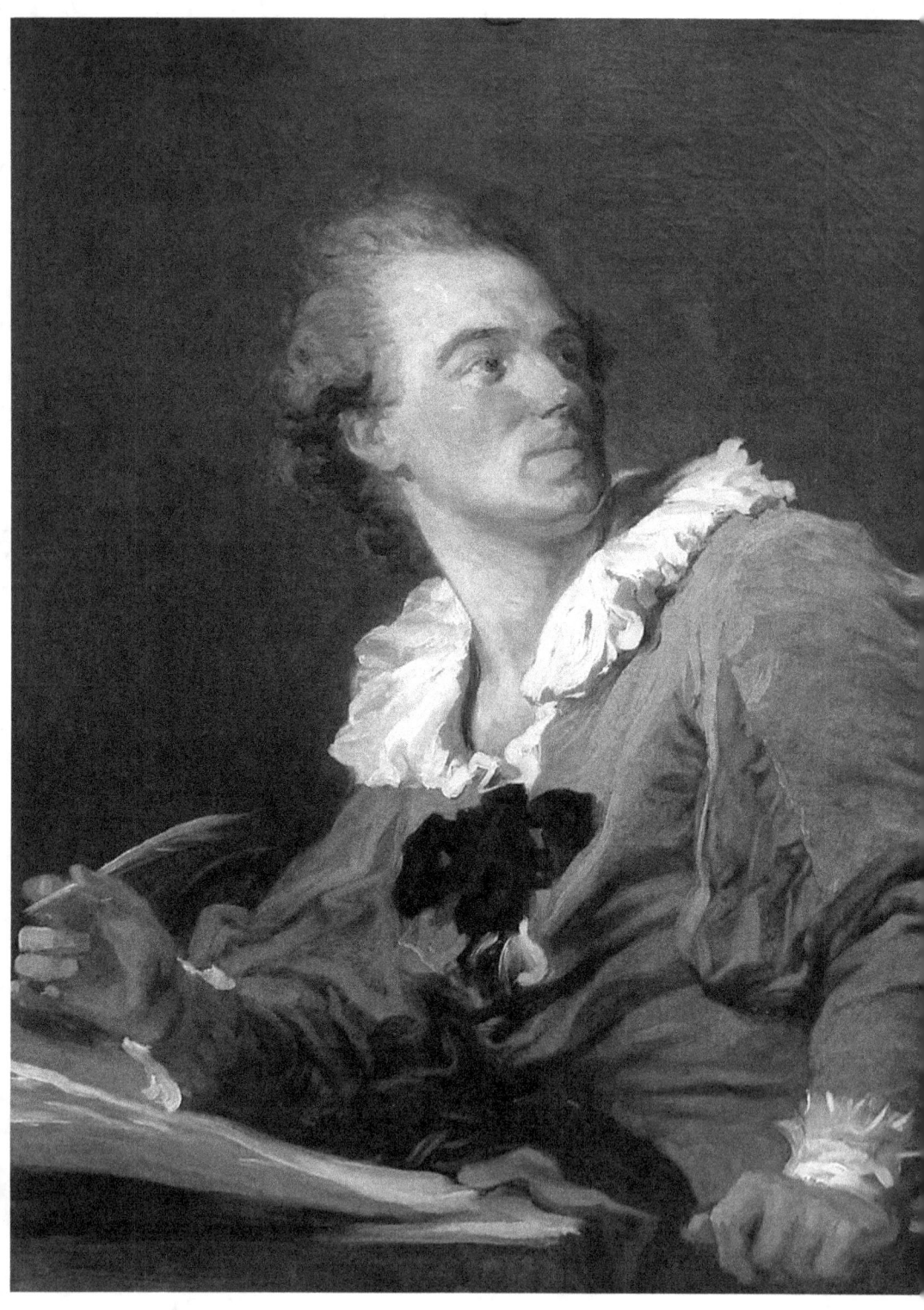

Jean Honoré Fragonard, Inspiration, 1769

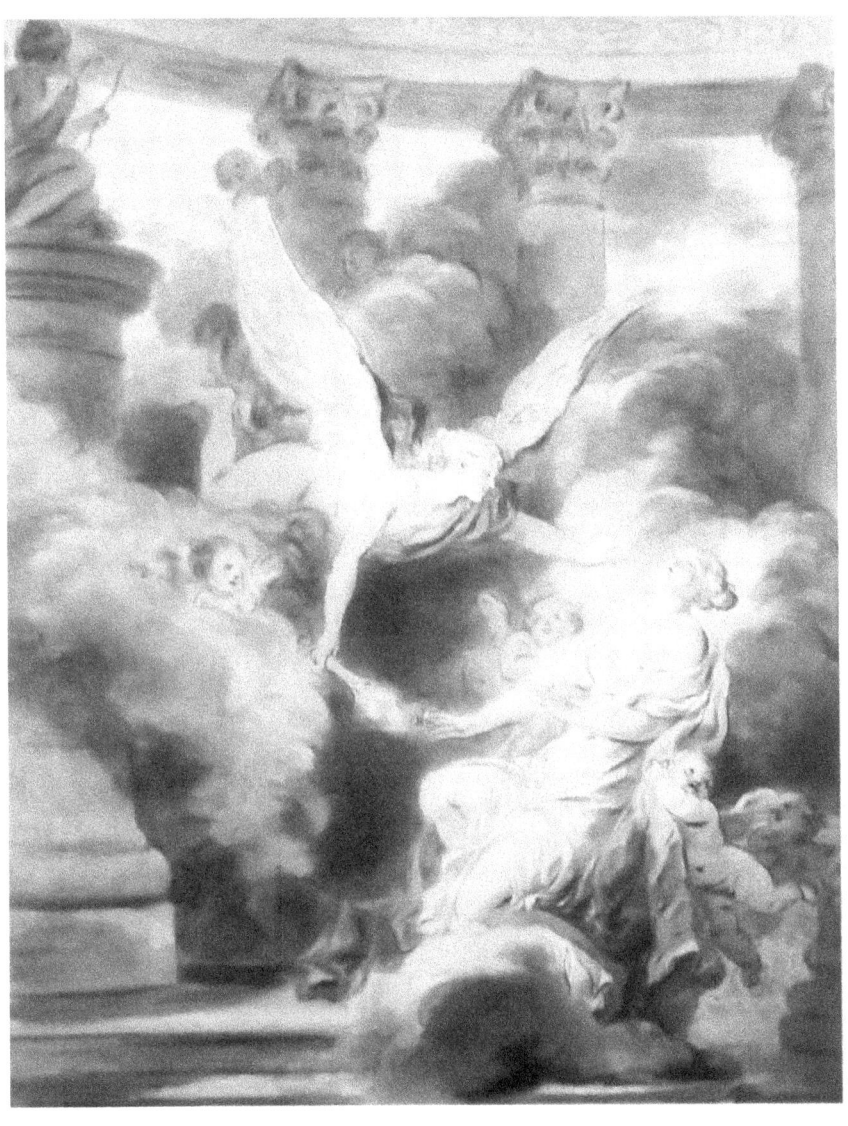

Jean-Honoré Fragonard, The Sacrifice of the Rose, c. 1780,
private collection

IV

MARRIAGE

There lived in Grasse, with its rich harvests of flowers, and given to the distilling of perfumes therefrom, a family that had come from Avignon – its name, Gérard, and on friendly terms with the Fragonards. It so chanced that a young woman of the family, the seventeen-year-old Marie Anne Gérard, was sent to Paris, to the care of Fragonard, in order to earn her living in the shop of a scent-seller, one Isnard. The girl had artistic leanings, and fell a-painting of fans and miniatures. She had need of a teacher; and who better qualified for the business than her townsman, the famous Fragonard? What more natural than that Fragonard should become her master? She was a jovial girl. So they would talk of home, and the people amongst whom they had been bred. She was no particular beauty, as her picture by Fragonard proves; she had the rough accent of Provence; was thick-set and clumsy of figure, and of heavy features, but she had the youth and freshness and health of a young woman's teens, that hide the blemishes and full significance of these coarsenesses. She and Fragonard fell a-kissing. Fragonard, now thirty-seven, married Marie Anne Gérard in her eighteenth year; and she bore him a much loved daughter, Rosalie – and ten years later, in 1780, a son, Alexandre Evariste Fragonard.

There came to live with the newly married couple his wife's younger sister Marguerite and her young brother Henri Gérard, who was learning engraving.

Fragonard's marriage at once affected his habits and his art. The wild oats of his artistic career were near sown. The naughtinesses of girls of pleasure gave place to the grace and tenderness of the home-life – the cradle took the place of the bed of light adventures; and children blossomed on to his canvases. He set aside the make-believe shepherds and shepherdesses of the vogue; and henceforth painted the "real thing" in rural surroundings.

He brought to his homeliest pictures a beauty of arrangement, a sense of style, and a dignity worthy of the most majestic subjects. He came at this time under the influence of the Dutch landscapists, and stole from them the solidity of their massing in foliage, the truth of their character-drawing, the close observation of their cattle and animal-life, their cloudy skies, and the finish and force of their craftsmanship. Whether he went into Holland is disputed. He was too keen an artist, his was too original a genius, to imitate their style or take on their Dutch accent. He simply took from them such part of their craftsmanship as could enter into the facile gracious genius of France without clogging its grace. He is now content with his house and garden for scenery, with his family for models. He realises that an artist has no need to go abroad to find "paintable things."

The "Heureuse Fécondité," the "Visit to the Nurse" (the second one), the "Schoolmistress," the "Good Mother," the "Retour au logis," the "L'Education fait tout," the "Dites donc, si'l vous plaît," are of this period.

In all he did he proves himself an artist, incapable of mediocrity, bringing distinction and style to all that he touches.

Fragonard also excelled in the painting of miniatures. And there are small portraits under fancy names to be seen at the Louvre, painted with a breadth and force that prove him to have known the work of Franz Hals. The figure of a man, known as "Figure de Fantaisie" or "Inspiration," is stated with a directness and vividness worthy of the great Dutch master. Indeed, there is much in the direct handling of the paint and the life of the thing that recalls Franz Hals – the very arrangement of the dress and the treatment of the hand being a careless attempt to recall the habits and fashions of the Dutchman. "La Musique" repeats the impression. And even the more pronouncedly French style of the pretty woman in "La Chanteuse" does not disguise the inspiration of Franz Hals in the painting of the bodice, the cuffs, and the details – the high ruffle is "dragged in" from Hals's day. The "Music Lesson" at the Louvre was painted about the same time.

Fragonard's old master, Boucher, for some time had been "going about like a shadow of himself." The year after Fragonard's marriage the old painter was found dead, sitting at his easel before an unfinished picture of Venus, the brush fallen out of his fingers – the light of the "Glory of Paris" gone out.

Boucher died a few months before that Christmas Eve of 1770 that saw Choiseul driven from power by the trio of knaves who used the vulgar but kindly woman Du Barry as their tool – indeed she refused to pull the great minister down until she had made handsome terms on his behalf; Choiseul was too astute a man not to recognise what lay beyond the shadow of her pretty skirts – nay, does he not turn in the courtyard as he leaves the palace to go into banishment, his *lettre de cachet* in his pocket, and, seeing a woman looking out from a window at the end of an alley, bow and kiss his hand to the window where gazes out of tear-filled eyes this strange doomed beauty who has won to the sceptre of France? 'Twas four years before the small-pox took the king – four years during which this same Du Barry, with her precious trio, d'Aiguillon, Maupeou, and Terray, sent the members of Parliament into banishment – years that launched royal France on its downward rushing, with laughter and riot, to its doom, whilst the apathetic Louis shrugged his now gross royal shoulders at all warnings of catastrophe, which to give him due credit, he was scarce witless enough or blind enough not to foresee. Nay, did he not even admit it in his constantly affirmed, if cynical, creed that "things, as they were, would last as long as he; and he that came after him must shift for himself"? Ay; he came even nearer to the kernel of the significance of things, when, shrugging his no longer well-beloved shoulders, as the Pompadour had done, he repeated her cynical saying of "*Après nous le déluge.*" It was to be a deluge indeed – scarlet red.

Wit and ruthless fatuity were the order of the day; these folk were wondrous full of the neatly turned phrase and the polished epigram. Most fatuous of them all, and as ruthless as any, was Terray – he who tinkered with finance, with crown to his many infamies the scandalous *Pacte de Famille*, that mercantile company that was to produce an artificial rise in the price of corn by buying up the grain of France, exporting it, and bringing it back for sale at vast profit – with Louis of France as considerable shareholder. Had not the owners of the land the right to do what they would with their own? 'Twas small wonder that the well-beloved became the highly-detested of the groaning people – he and his precious privileged class.

Yet Louis of France spake prophecy – if unwitting of it. The guillotine was not to have him. In 1774 he was stricken down with the small-pox, and the sick-room in the palace saw the Du Barry and her party fight a duel with Choiseul's party for his possession – never, surely, was a more grim, more fantastic warfare than that bitter intrigue to get the confessor to the king's bedside, that meant the dismissal of the favourite before he should be allowed to receive the Absolution – in which the strange blasphemy was enacted of the Eucharist being hustled about the passages, whilst the bigots strove against its administration, and the freethinkers demanded the last consolation of the Church. On the 10th of May the small-pox took his distempered body, "already a mass of corruption," that was hastily flung into a coffin and hurried without pomp, or circumstance, or pretence of honours to St. Denis – being rattled thereto at the trot, the crowd that lined the way showering epigrams not wholly friendly upon its passing; and was buried amongst the bones of the ancient kings of his race, unattended by the Court, and amidst the contempt and loud curses of his people.

Even the poor weeping Du Barry was gone, hustled from the palace at the wandering orders of the dying delirious king. D'Aiguillon also, and Maupeou and Terray were gone. And the Court was hailing the new king and his queen – ill-fated Louis the Sixteenth and tactless Marie Antoinette.

The scandalous levity of the privileged class of the day, and its ruthless vindictiveness when thwarted, had near done their work. A proud and gallant people touched bottom in humiliation. The pens of the wits and thinkers sent the new opinion broadcast amongst a people wholly scandalised and punished by the corruption of their governors. These writings made astounding and alarming way. The "intellectuals" were all on the side of the people – Montesquieu, Voltaire, Diderot, Rousseau, d'Alembert, Helvetius, Condillac, the Abbé Raynal. With wit and sarcasm and invective and argument, they stirred passions, appealing to self-respect and dignity and honour and the innate love of freedom in the strong; they appealed to common-sense, to the craving for liberty in man's being, to the rights of the individual; and the printing-press scattered their wit and wisdom throughout the land to the uttermost corners of France. They sneered away false aristocracy, false religion. They wrought to overthrow the old order, and brought it into contempt. And they needed to manufacture no evidence. France had lain supine, a mighty people as they proved themselves when their right arms were freed – lain in chains under the heel of a king who had been capable of setting their necks under the feet of a trivial and foolish woman, whose nursery had been the gutter.

Yet Du Barry, when all her faults are set against her, suffered undue execration. She had no grain of ill-will in her nature. During her reign the Bastille received no prisoner at her ordering – vengeance was not in her. She was the tool of unscrupulous men; but she came between them and their base vengeances, and kept the Court free from the brutalities that the Pompadour meted out to her enemies without a pang of remorse. During the whole of her reign, she visited her old mother every fortnight, and lavished benefits on her kin – whom most women, thus suddenly raised to the noblesse, would have avoided like a plague. The scoundrels who made her their toy were responsible for every evil deed that she was accused of committing. And even the new king, whose sharp *lettre de cachet*, written two days after he came to the throne, banished her to a convent, soon relented, and allowed her to go back to her home at Luciennes. The Du Barry had striven to abolish the *lettre de cachet*; the new king brought it back, inaugurating his reign by having one sent to the woman whose gentleness and kindliness had shrunk from the accursed thing. It was a fit omen of the well-meaning but incompetent king's tragic reign which was about to begin.

To Fragonard these things were but tattle; yet the doing of them was to reach to his hearth; the consequences of them were to strip him bare and wreck him – he was to see his wife and womenkind dragging through the streets of Paris to beg bread and meat at the gates of the city. But the future was mercifully hidden from him. He was now at the height of his career; and was to taste wider success.

Fragonard's name will always be linked with that of his friend and patron, a wealthy man, the farmer-general Bergeret de Grandcour. His family visited at the rich man's houses in town and country.

Now the career of a rich man was incomplete without the making of the Grand Tour. At the least the gentleman of means must have roamed through Italy. And it was thus that, with Bergeret de Grandcour, Fragonard now made his second journey into Italy in his forty-second year.

Fragonard was delighted at the prospect of seeing his loved Italy again after twelve years. It was a family party – Fragonard and his wife, with Bergeret de Grandcour and his son, to say nothing of Bergeret's servants and cook and following. It was a happy, merry journeying in extravagant luxury.

Fragonard had aforetime gone into Italy as a penniless student and an unknown man; he now travelled in the grand style as the guest of a man of affairs, visiting palaces and churches, received in state by the highest in the land, dining with the Ambassador of France, having audience of the Pope, advising Bergeret de Grandcour in the buying of art-treasures. He tasted all the delights of great wealth. He went to a concert "chez le lord Hamilton," seeing and speaking with *la belle Emma* – Nelson's Emma. He stood in Naples; he tramped up Vesuvius. It was at Naples the news came that Louis the Fifteenth lay dying of the small-pox – a few days later the old king died.

The party at once turned their faces homewards, returning to Paris in leisurely fashion by way of Venice, Vienna, and Germany, only to know, at the journey's ending, one of those miserable and sordid quarrels that seem to dog the friendships of men of genius. Going to Bergeret de Grandcour's house in Paris to get his portfolios of sketches, made throughout the journey, Fragonard found to his amazement and consternation that Bergeret de Grandcour angrily refused to give them up, claiming them as payment for his outlay upon him during the Italian journey. The sorry business ended in the law-courts, and in the loss of the lawsuit by Bergeret de Grandcour, who was condemned to give up the drawings or to pay a 30,000 livres fine (£6000). The ugly breach that threatened to open between them, however, was soon healed by reconciliation; and Bergeret de Grandcour's son became one of Fragonard's closest and most intimate friends.

V

THE TERROR

Louis the Sixteenth, third son of the Dauphin who had been Louis the Fifteenth's only lawful son, ascended the throne in his twentieth year, a pure-minded young fellow, full of good intentions, sincerely anxious for the well-being of his people; but of a diffident and timid character, and under the influence of a young consort, the beautiful Queen Marie Antoinette, of imperious temper and of light and frivolous manners, who brought to her counsels a deplorable lack of judgment.

The Du Barry sent a-packing, and d'Aiguillon and the rest of their crew, the young king recalled the crafty old Maurepas who had been banished by the Pompadour, an ill move – though the setting of Turgot over the finances augured well. And when the great minister Turgot fell, he gave way to as good a man, the worthy honest banker, Neckar.

In a happy hour Fragonard was granted by the king the eagerly sought haven of the artists of his time – a studio and apartments at the old palace of the Louvre, as his master Boucher had been granted them before him.

Settling in with his wife, his girl Rosalie, his son Alexandre Evariste, and his talented sister-in-law Marguerite Gérard, he lived thereat a life almost opulent, making large sums of money, some eight thousand pounds a year, at this time. He joyed in decorating his rooms. He was the life and soul of a group of brilliant men who gathered about him, having the deepest affection for him.

His sister-in-law, Marguerite Gérard, was as gay and distinguished in manners, and as beautiful, as his jovial wife was dull and vulgar and coarse – the vile accent of Grasse, that made his wife's speech horrible to the ear, becoming slurred into a shadow of itself on Marguerite's tongue, and turned by the enchanting accents of the younger sister's lips into seduction. This girl's friendship and companionship became an ever-increasing delight to the aging painter. Their correspondence, when apart, was passionately affectionate. Ugly scandals got abroad – scandals difficult to prove or disprove. The man and woman were of like tastes, of like temperaments; it was, likely enough, little more than that. The girl was of a somewhat cold nature; and we must read her last letters as censoriously as her first – when, in reply to Fragonard, evil days having fallen upon him, and being old and next to ruined, on his asking her for money to help him, she, who owed everything to him, refused him with the trite sermon: "to practise economy, to be reasonable, and to remember that in brooding over fancies one only increases them without being any the happier." But this was not as yet.

Fragonard, happy in his home at the Louvre, free from cares, content amongst devoted friends, reached his fifty-fifth year when he had suddenly to gaze horrified at the first ugly hint that, in the years to come, he must expect to hear the scythe of the Great Reaper – know the passing of friends and loved ones. He was to reel under the first serious blow of his life. His bright, witty, winsome girl Rosalie died in her eighteenth year. It nearly killed him.

But there was a blacker, a vaster shadow came looming over the land – a threat that boded ill for such as took life too airily.

In an unfortunate moment for the royal house, and against the will of the king and of Neckar, the nation went mad with enthusiasm over England's revolted American colonies; and the alliance was formed that France swore not to sever until America was declared independent. It started the war with England. The successes of the revolted colonies made the coming of the Revolution in France a certainty. The fall of Neckar and the rise of the new minister, Calonne, sent France rushing to the brink. The distress of the people became unbearable. The royal family and the Court sank in the people's respect, and the people were no longer the people of the decade before – they had watched the Revolution in America, and they had seen the Revolution victorious. The fall of Calonne only led to the rise of the turbulent and stupid Cardinal de Brienne; and the Court was completely foul of the people when De Brienne threw up office in a panic and fled across the frontier, leaving the Government in utter confusion.

The king recalled Neckar. The calling of the States-General now became assured. Paris rang with the exultation of the Third Estate.

The States-General met at Versailles on the 5th of May 1789. The monarchy was at an end. In little over a month the States-General created itself the National Assembly. The Revolution was begun. The 14th of July saw the fall of the Bastille. On the 22nd the people hanged Foulon to the street-lamp at the corner of the Place de Grève – and *à la lanterne!* became the cry of fashion.

Fragonard was in his fifty-seventh year when he heard in his lodging at the Louvre the thunderclap of this 14th of July 1789 – saw the dawn of the Revolution.

The rose of the dawn was soon to turn to blood-red crimson. The storm had been muttering and growling its curses for years before the death of Louis the Fifteenth. It came up in threatening blackness darkly behind the dawn, and was soon to break with a roar upon reckless Paris. It came responsive to the rattle of musketry in the far West, hard by Boston harbour.

Fragonard and his friends were of the independents – they

were liberals whom love of elegance had not prevented from sympathising with the sufferings of the people, and who had thrilled with the new thought. Fragonard's intelligence drew him naturally towards the new ideas; indeed he owed little to the Court; and when France was threatened by the coalition of Europe against her, he, with Gérard, David, and others, went on the 7th of September with the artist's womenfolk to give up their jewelry to the National Assembly.

But the storm burst, and soon affairs became tragic red.

There came, for the ruin of the cause of a constitutional monarchy and to end the last hope of the Court party, the unfortunate death of Mirabeau – the hesitations of the king – his foolish flight to Varennes – his arrest.

The constitutional party in the Legislative Assembly, at first dominant, became subordinate to the more violent but more able *Girondists*, with their extreme wing of *Jacobins* under Robespierre, and *Cordeliers* under Danton, Marat, Camille Desmoulins, and Fabre d'Eglantine. The proscription of all emigrants quickly followed. It was as unsafe to leave as to stay in Paris. The queen's insane enmity towards Lafayette finished the king's business. On the night of the 9th of August the dread tocsin sounded the note of doom to the royal cause – herald to the bloodshed of the morrow. Three days afterwards, the king and the royal family were prisoners in the Temple.

The National Convention met for the first time on the 21st of September 1792; decreed the First Year of the Republic, abolished Royalty and the titles of courtesy, decreed in their place *citoyen* and *citoyenne*, and the use of *tu* and *toi* for *vous*.

The National Convention also displayed the antagonism of the two wings of the now all-powerful Girondist party – the Girondists and the Jacobins or Montagnards. The conflict began with the quarrel as to whether the king could be tried. The 10th of January 1793 saw the king's head fall to the guillotine – the Jacobins had triumphed. War with Europe followed, and the deadly struggle between the Girondists and Jacobins for supreme power. The 27th of May 1793 witnessed the appointment of the terrible and secret Committee of Public Safety. By June the Girondists had wholly fallen. Charlotte Corday's stabbing of Marat in his bath left the way clear for Robespierre's ambition. The Jacobins in power, the year of the Reign of Terror began – July 1793 to July 1794 – with Robespierre as the lord of the hellish business. The scaffolds reeked with blood – from that of Marie Antoinette and Egalité Orleans to that of the Girondist deputies and Madame Roland, and the most insignificant beggar suspected of the vague charge of "hostility to the Republic." In a mad moment the Du Barry, who had shown the noblest side of her character in befriending the old allies of her bygone days of greatness, published a notice of a theft from her house. It drew all eyes to her wealth. And she went to the guillotine shrieking with terror and betraying all who had protected her. Then came strife amongst the Jacobins. Robespierre and Danton fought the scoundrel Hébert for life, and overthrew him. The Hebertists went to the guillotine, dying in abject terror. Danton, with his appeals for cessation of the bloodshed of the Terror, alone stood between Robespierre and supreme power. Danton, Camille Desmoulins, Eglantine and their humane fellows, were sent to the guillotine. Between the 10th of June and the 27th of July, in 1794, fourteen hundred people in Paris alone died on the scaffold.

Fragonard dreaded to fly from the tempest. It was as safe to remain in Paris as to leave the city. Any day he might be taken. Sadness fell upon him and ate into his heart. The old artist could not look without uneasiness upon the ruin of the aristocracy, of the farmers-general, and of the gentle class, now in exile or prison or under trial – his means of livelihood utterly gone. Without hate for Royalty or for the Republic, the artists, by birth plebeian and in manners bourgeois, many of them old men, could but blink with fearful eyes at the vast upheaval. Their art was completely put out of fashion – a new art, solemn and severe, classical and heroic, was born. For half a century the charming art of France of the eighteenth century lay wholly buried – a thing of contempt wherever it showed above the ashes.

Fragonard's powerful young friend David, the painter, now stood sternly watchful over the old man's welfare; and David was at the height of his popularity – he was a member of the Convention. He took every opportunity to show his friendship publicly, visited Fragonard regularly, secured him his lodgings at the Louvre, brought about his election to the jury of the Arts created by the Convention to take the place of the Royal Academy.

But the old artist was bewildered.

The national enthusiasm was not in him. The artists were ruined by the destruction of their pensions. The buyers of Fragonard's pictures were dispersed, their power and their money gone, their favour dissipated. Fragonard worked on without conviction or truth. The new school uprooted all his settled ideals. He struggled hard to catch the new ideas, and failed. He helped to plant a tree of liberty in the court of the Louvre, meditating the while how he could be gone from Paris – it was a tragic farce, played with his soul. The glories of the Revolution alarmed the old man. He saw the kinsfolk of his friends dragged off to the guillotine. He had guarded against suspicion and arrest by giving a certificate early in 1794, the year of the Terror, stating that he had no intention of emigrating, adding a statement of residence, and avowing his citizenship. He felt that even these acts were not enough protection in these terrible years. No man knew when or where the blow might fall – at what place or moment he might be seized, or on what charge, and sent to the guillotine. Friends were taken in the night. Hubert Robert was seized and flung into Saint Lazare, escaping death but by an accident. The state of misery and want amongst the artists and their wives and families at this time was pitiable.

Fragonard gladly snatched at the invitation of an old friend of his family, Monsieur Maubert, to go to him at Grasse during these anxious times of the travail that had come upon France.

Shortly after that Sunday in December when the Du Barry

went shrieking to her hideous death at the guillotine, Fragonard, turning his face to the South of his birth, was rolling up amongst his baggage the four finished canvases of "The Romance of Love and Youth," and the unfinished fifth canvas, "Deserted," ordered and repudiated by the Du Barry. He bundled his family into a chaise, and lumbered out of Paris, rumbling on clattering wheels through the guards at the gates, and making southwards towards Provence for his friend's house at Grasse. Here, far away from the din and strife, Fragonard set up his world-famous decorative panels in the salon of his host, which they admirably fitted, painting for the overdoors, "Love the Conqueror," "Love-folly," "Love pursuing a Dove," "Love embracing the Universe," and a panel over the fireplace, "Triumph of Love." He also painted during his stay the portraits of the brothers Maubert; and, to keep his host safe from ugly rumours and unfriendly eyes, he decorated the vestibule with revolutionary emblems, phrygian bonnet, axes and faggots, and the masks of Robespierre and the Abbé Gregoire, and the like trickings of red republicanism.... His host was the maternal grandfather of the Malvilan, at whose death in 1903, the room and its decorations were sold to an American collector for a huge sum of money.

Meanwhile, able and resolute men had determined that Robespierre and the Terror must end. Robespierre went to the guillotine. The Revolution of the Ninth Thermidor put an end to the Terror in July 1794.

All this time the armies of France were winning the respect of the world by their gallantry and skill. The 23rd of September 1795, saw France establish the Directory – the 5th of October, the Day of the Sections, saw the stiff fight about the Church of St. Roch, and Napoleon Bonaparte appointed second-in-command of the army. The young general was soon Commander-in-Chief. And France thenceforth advanced, spite of the many blunders of the Directory, with all the genius of her race, to the splendid recovery of her fortunes, and to a greatness which was to be the wonder and admiration and dread of the world.

The Revolution of the 18th and 19th of Brumaire (9th and 10th of November 1799) destroyed the Directory and set the people's idol, Napoleon Bonaparte, at the helm of her mighty state.

VI

THE END

To Paris Fragonard crept back, he and his family, to his old quarters at the Louvre, when Napoleon was come to power, and the guillotine was slaked with blood. He returned to Paris a poor old man.

The enthusiasm was gone out of his invention, the volition out of his hand's cunning, the breath out of his career. He was out of the fashion; a man risen from the dead. His efforts to catch the spirit of the time were pathetic. He painted rarely now. He won a passing success with an historic canvas or so, done in the new manner. But what did Fragonard know of political allegories? what enthusiasm had he for the famous days of the Revolution? what were caricature or satire to him, any more than the heroic splendour of Greece and Rome? The gods of elegance were dead; a severe and frigid morality stood upon their altars.

We have a pen-picture of the old painter at this time – short, big of head, stout, full-bodied, brisk, alert, ever gay; he has red cheeks, sparkling eyes, grey hair very much frizzed out; he is to be seen wandering about the Louvre dressed in a cloak or overcoat of a mixed grey cloth, without hooks or eyes or buttons – a cloak which the old man, when he is at work, ties at the waist with it does not matter what – a piece of string, a crumpled chiffon. Every one loves "little father Fragonard." Through every shock of good and evil fortune he remains alert and cheerful. The old face smiles even through tears.

Thus, walking with aging step towards the end, he saw Napoleon created Emperor of the French, his triumphant career marred only at rare intervals by such disasters as Trafalgar – heard perhaps of the suicide of the unfortunate but gallant Villeneuve at the disgrace of trial by court-martial for this very loss of Trafalgar.

In the year of 1806, on the New Year's Day of which were abolished the Republican reckonings of the years as established at the Revolution, suddenly came the suppression of the artists' lodging at the Louvre by decree of the Emperor. The Fragonards went to live hard by in the house of the restaurant-keeper Very, in the Rue Grenelle Saint-Honoré. The move was for Fragonard but the prelude to a longer journey.

The old artist walks now more sluggishly than of old, his four-and-seventy years have taken the briskness out of his step. Returning from the Champ de Mars on a sultry day in August he becomes heated – enters a café to eat an ice; congestion of the brain sets in. At five of the clock in the morning of the 22nd day of August 1806, Fragonard enters into the eternal sleep – at the hour that his master Boucher had gone to sleep.

Thus passed away the last of the great painters of France's gaiety and lightness of heart.

Madame Fragonard lived to be seventy-seven, dying in 1824. Marguerite Gérard had a happy career as an artist under the Empire and the Restoration, but never married – dying at seventy-six, loaded with honours and in comfortable circumstances in the year that Queen Victoria came to the throne of England. Thus peacefully ended the days of Fragonard and his immediate kin after the turmoil and fierce tragic years of the Terror.

Painting with prodigal hand a series of elegant masterpieces in a century that made elegance its god, Fragonard disappeared, neglected and well-nigh discredited for years, with Watteau and Boucher and Greuze for goodly company; but with them, he is come into his own again, lord of a very realm of beauty.

To understand the atmosphere of the France of the seventeen-hundreds before the Revolution it is necessary to understand the art of Watteau, of Boucher, of Fragonard, and of Chardin. Of its pictured romance, Watteau and Boucher and Fragonard hold the keys. To shut the book of these is to be blind to the revelation of the greater part of that romance. Watteau states the new France of light airs and gaiety and pleasant prospects, tinged with sweet melancholy, that became the dream of a France rid of the pomposity and mock-heroics of the Grand Monarque; Boucher fulfils the century; Fragonard utters its swan's note. The art of Fragonard embodies astoundingly the pulsing evening of a century of the life of France, uttering its gay blithe note, skimming over the dangerous deeps of its mighty significance, yet not wholly disregarding the deeps as did the art of his two great forerunners. His is the last word of that mock-heroic France that Louis the Fourteenth built on stately and pompous pretence; that Louis the Fifteenth still further corrupted by the worship of mere elegance; that Louis the Sixteenth sent to its grave – a suffering people out of which a real France arose, from mighty and awful travail, like a giant, and stood bestriding the world, a superb reality.

NOTES ON WORKS

CHIFFRE D'AMOUR. Frontispiece
(In the Wallace Collection)

Fragonard, like his master Boucher, soon found that the pompous, historical, and religious pictures which the critics demanded of him, pleased no one but the critics. It was a fortunate day for him when he turned his back upon them, and employed his charming gifts upon the statement of the life of his day. And in few paintings that created his fame has he surpassed the fine handling of this scene, in which the girl cuts her lover's initials on the trunk of a tree – the dainty figure silhouetted against the dreamlike background of sky and tree that he loved so well. There is over all the glamour of the poetic statement supremely done.

THE MUSIC LESSON
(In the Louvre)

Fragonard had a profound admiration for the Dutch painters. Whether he went to Holland shortly after his marriage is not known; but he seems suddenly to have employed his brush as if he had come across fine examples of the Dutch school. "The Music Lesson" at the Louvre is one of these, and the Dutch influence is most marked both as to subject, treatment, and handling of the paint, if we allow for Fragonard's own strongly French personality.

L'ETUDE
(In the Louvre)

The picture of a young woman sometimes known as "L'Etude" (but perhaps better known as "La Chanteuse" or "Song") at the Louvre is another of those little canvases painted by Fragonard under the strong influence of the Dutch school, as we may see not only in the handling of the paint, and in the arrangement of the figure, but in the very ruffle about the girl's neck, the lace cuffs to the sleeves, and the treatment of the dress.

THE SCHOOLMISTRESS
(In the Wallace Collection)

After his marriage Fragonard's brush turned to the glorification of family life; and one of the most beautiful designs he conceived in this exquisite series was the picture of the schoolmistress and her small pupils – here chasteness of feeling has taken the place of levity; and purity of statement is evidenced even in the half-nude little fellow who is receiving his first lesson in culture.

FIGURE DE FANTASIE
(In the Louvre)

Here we have one of the rare examples of Fragonard's painting of a man's portrait. It is in strange contrast to his more delicate handling of domestic subjects.

LE VOEU À L'AMOUR
(In the Louvre)

This is an example of Fragonard in his grand-manner mood – a picture of the large decorative years that produced such masterpieces as the "Serment d'Amour," in which we see him ever interested above all things in the painting of bosky leafage and the dignity of great trees for background.

THE FAIR-HAIRED BOY
(In the Wallace Collection)

To the visitor to the Wallace collection the picture by Fragonard next best known after the "Chiffre d'Amour" and the "Swing," is this exquisite study of a fair-haired boy – the child is painted with a subtle grace and consummate delicacy rarely combined with the directness and impressionism here displayed by Fragonard.

LE BILLET DOUX

(In the Collection of M. Wildenstein, Paris)

Here we see Fragonard in his phase of sentimental recorder of love-scenes so typical of the art of Louis the Fifteenth's day.

On the following pages are illustrations of some of the contemporaries of Fragonard.

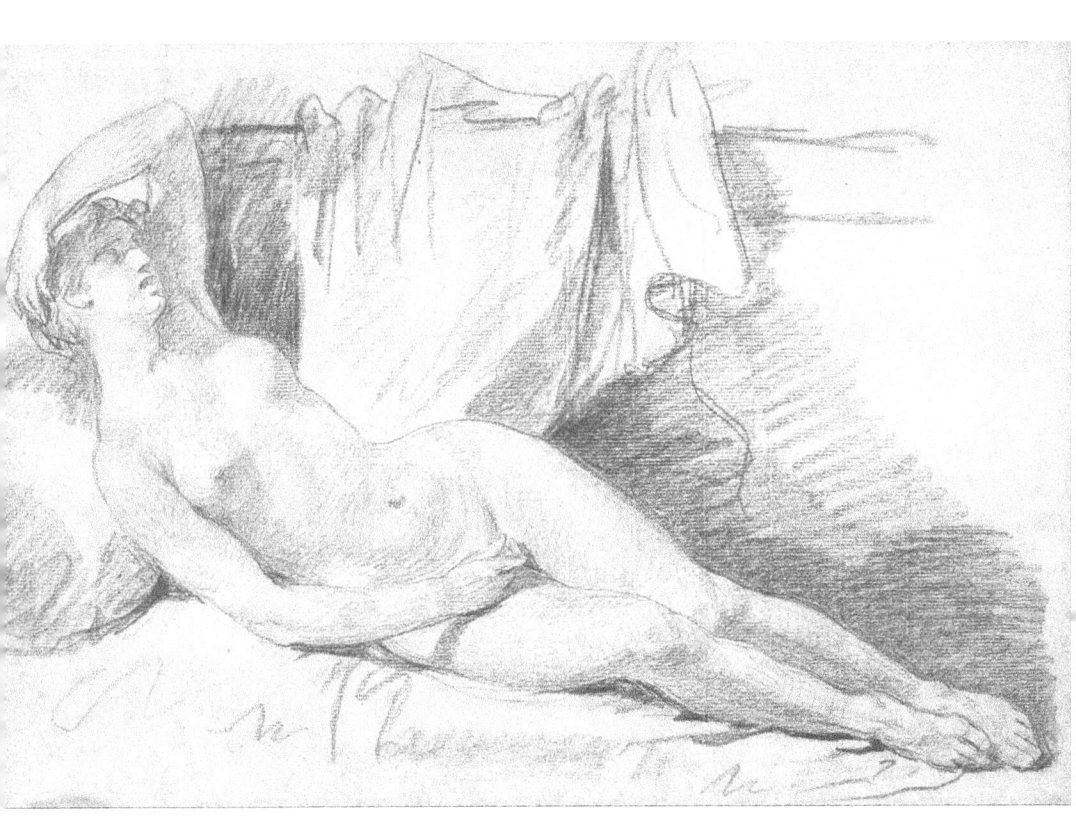

Jean-Baptiste Greuze, Reclining Female Nude,
Study For Aegina Visited By Jupiter, 1762-82

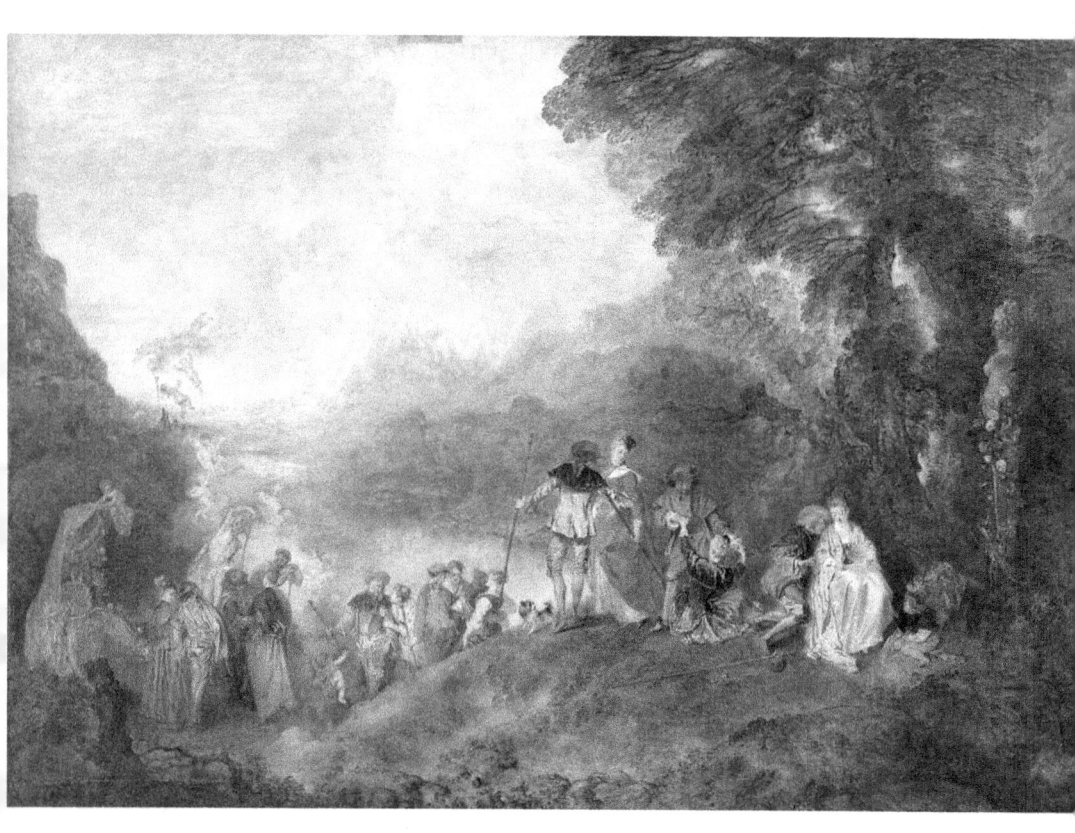

Jean-Antoine Watteau, L'Embarquement pour l'Ile de Cythere, 1717, Louvre, Paris

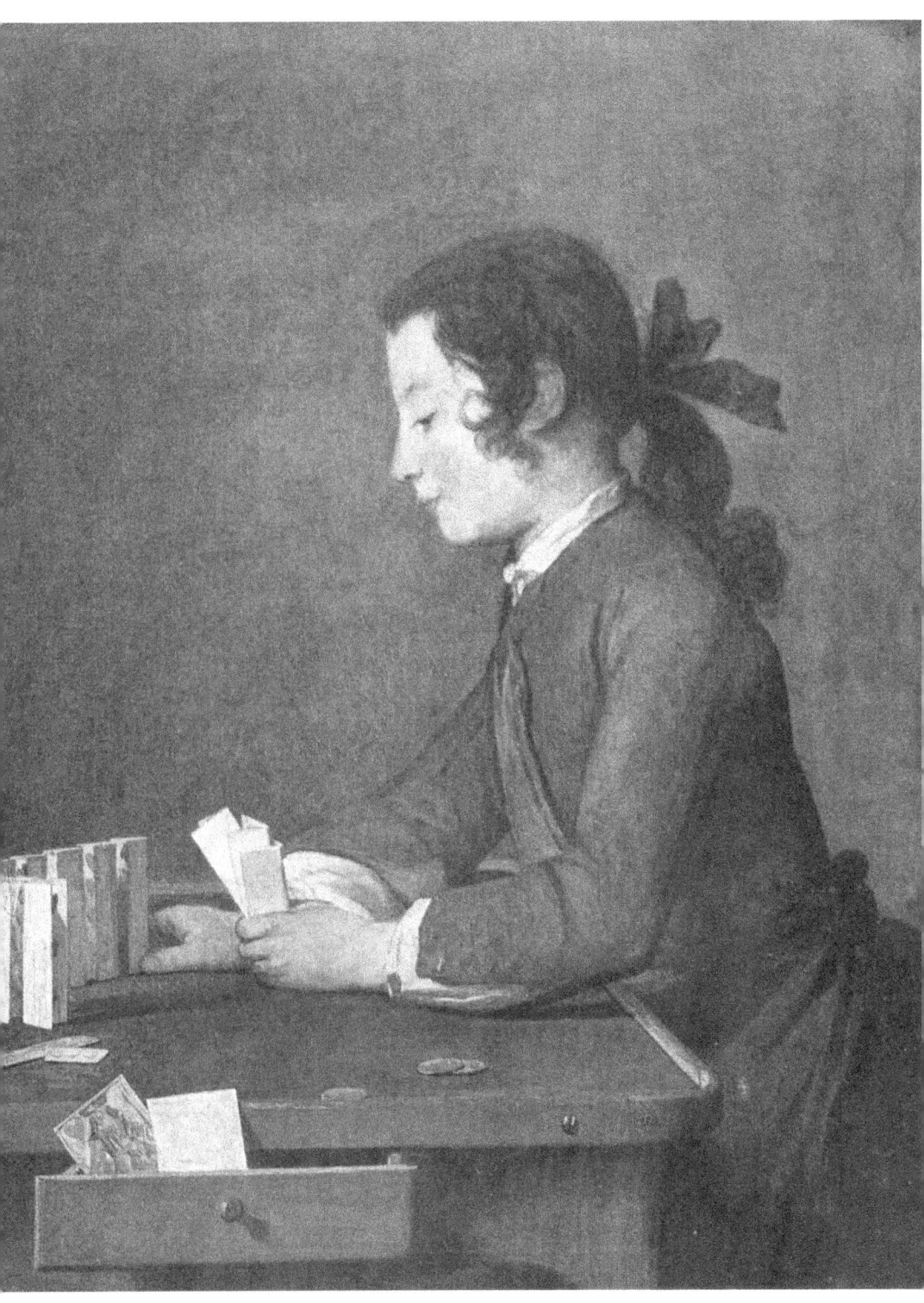

Jean-Baptiste Siméon Chardin, The House of Cards, 1735

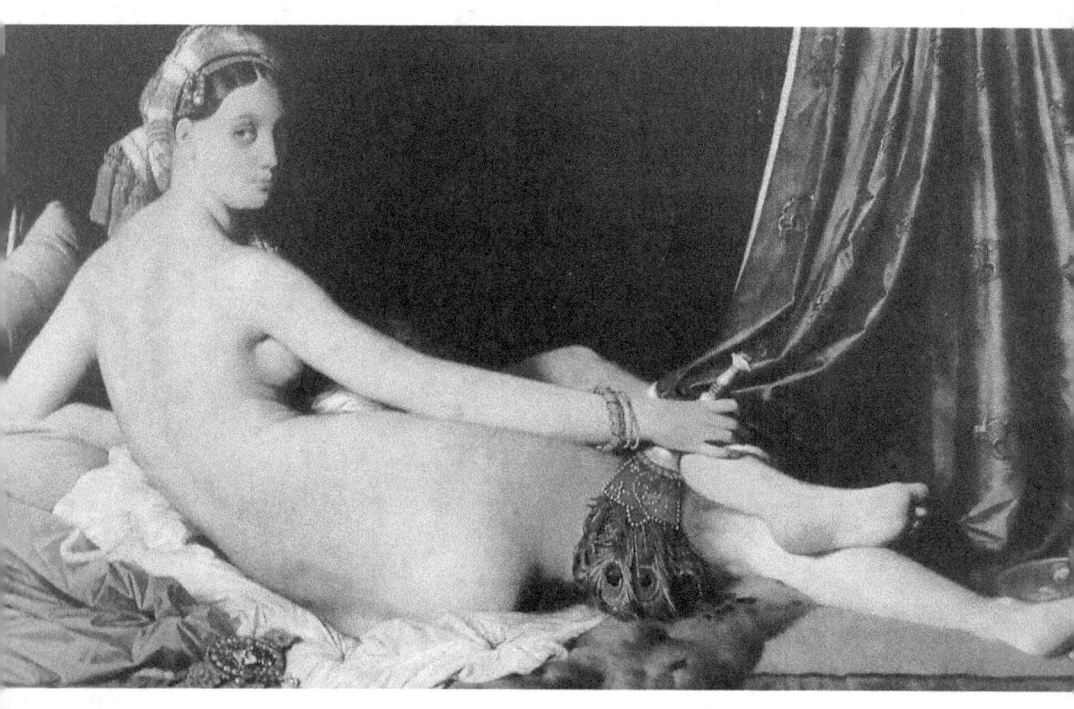

Jean-Dominique Ingres, Grand Odalisque, 1814

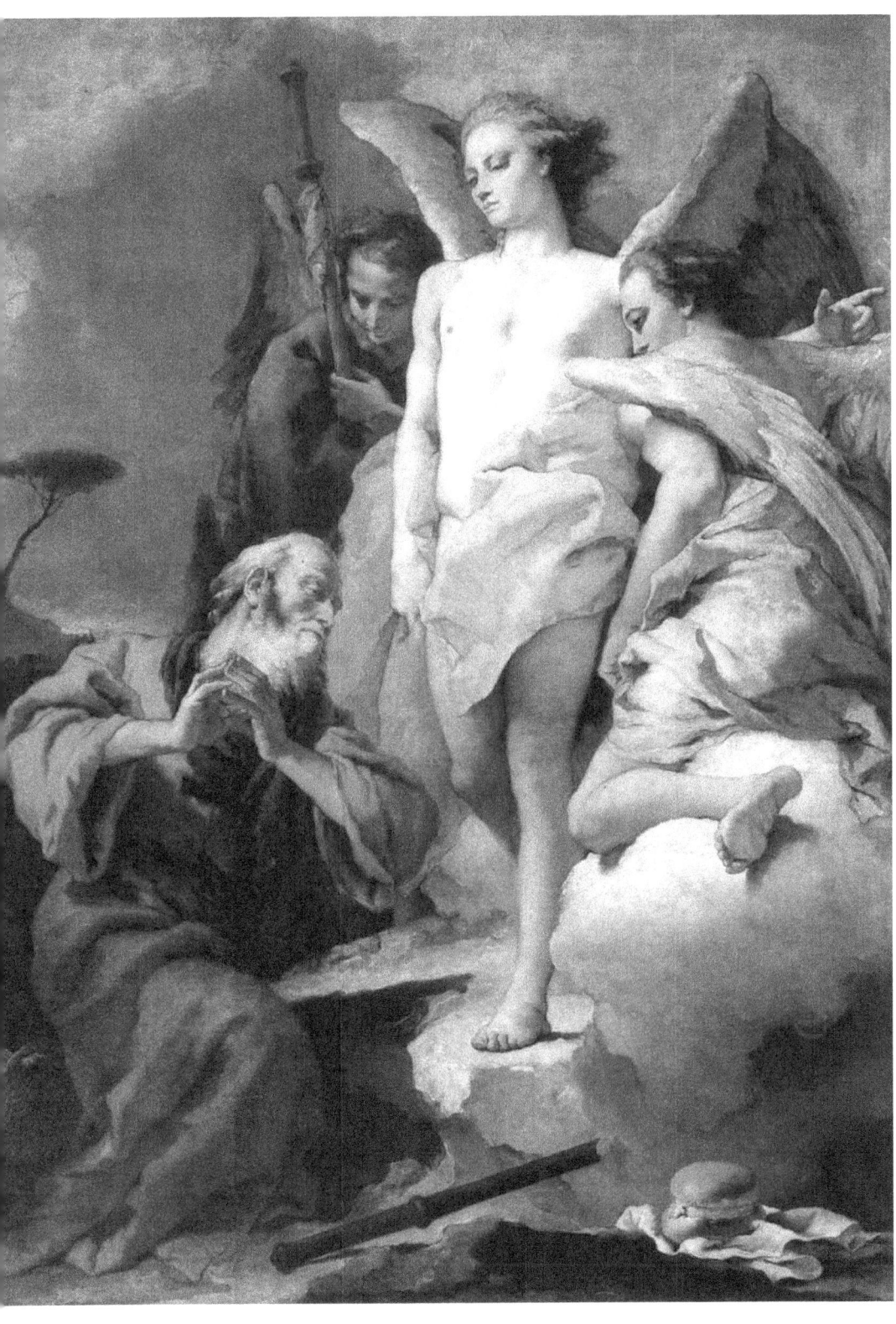

Giovanni Battista Tiepolo, Abraham and Three Angels, c. 1770

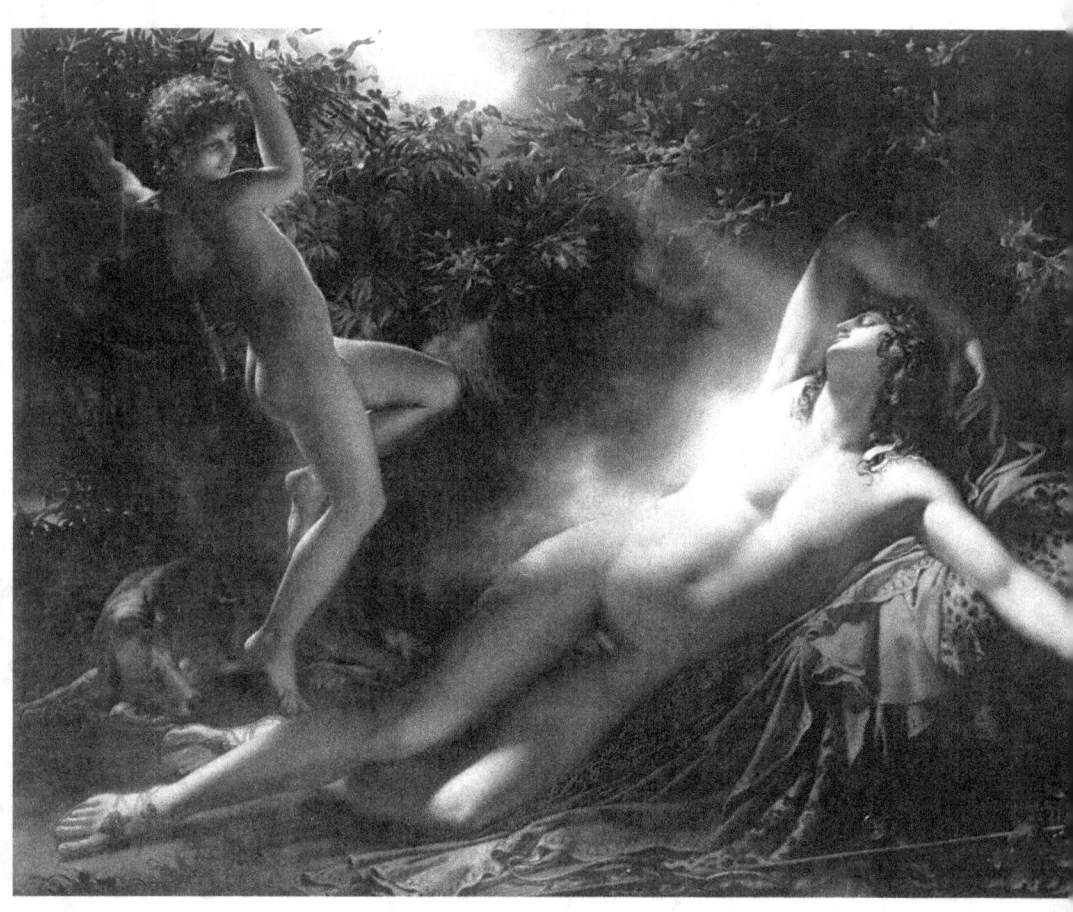

Anne-Louis Girodet-Trioson, Endymion, 1793

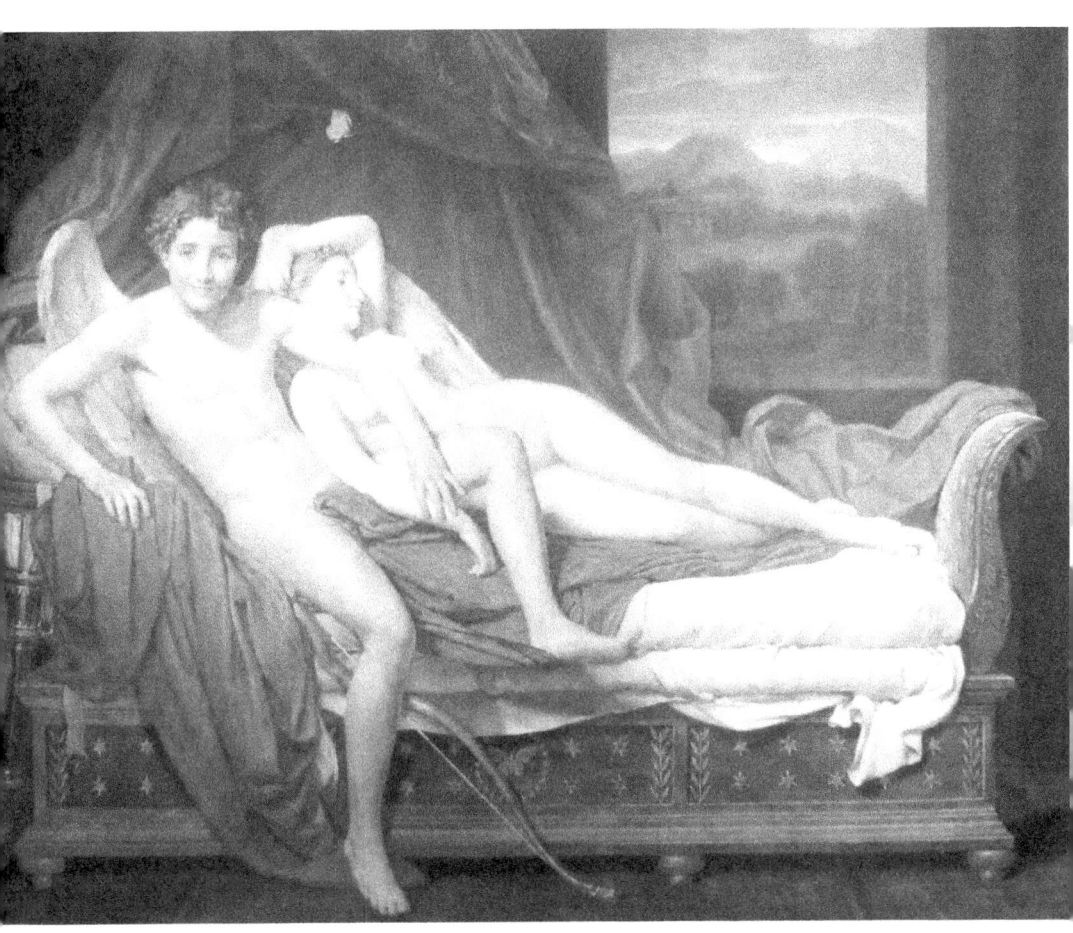

Jacques-Louis David, Cupid and Psyche, 1817,
Cleveland Museum of Art

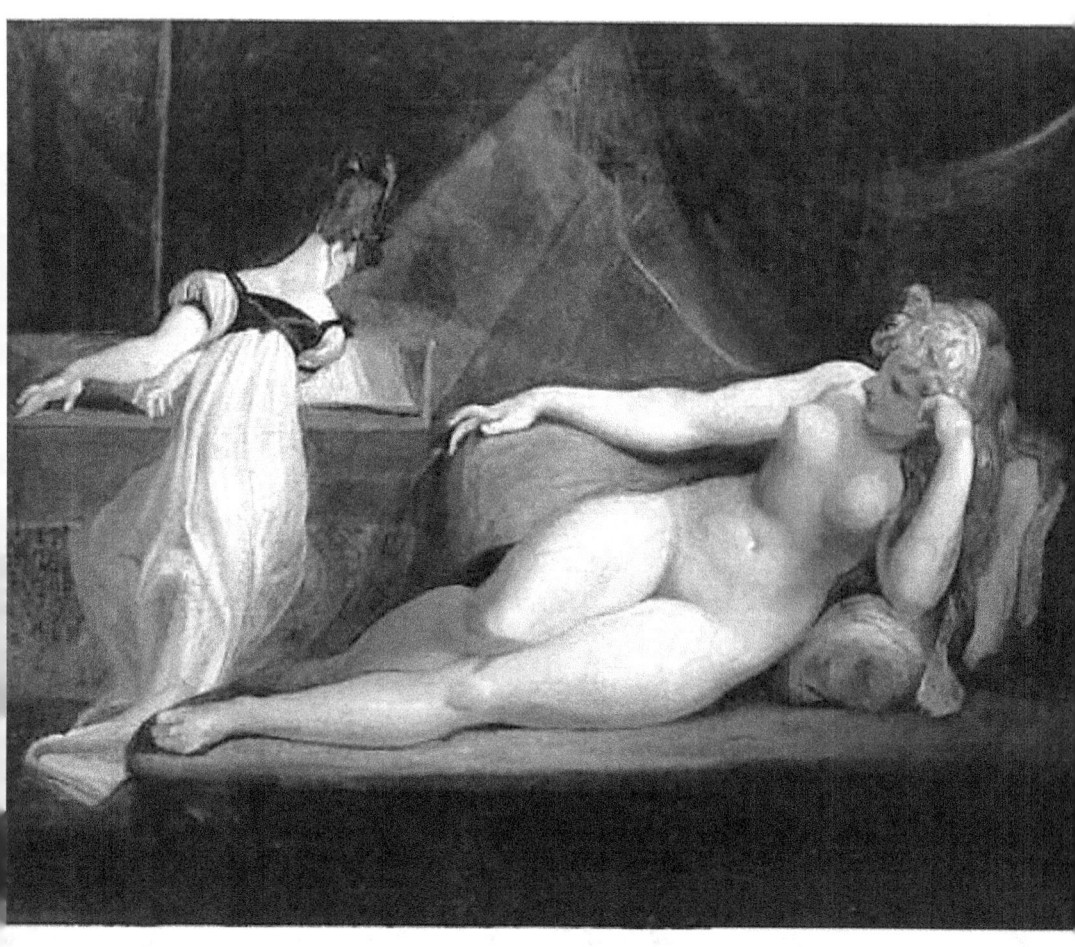

Henry Fuseli

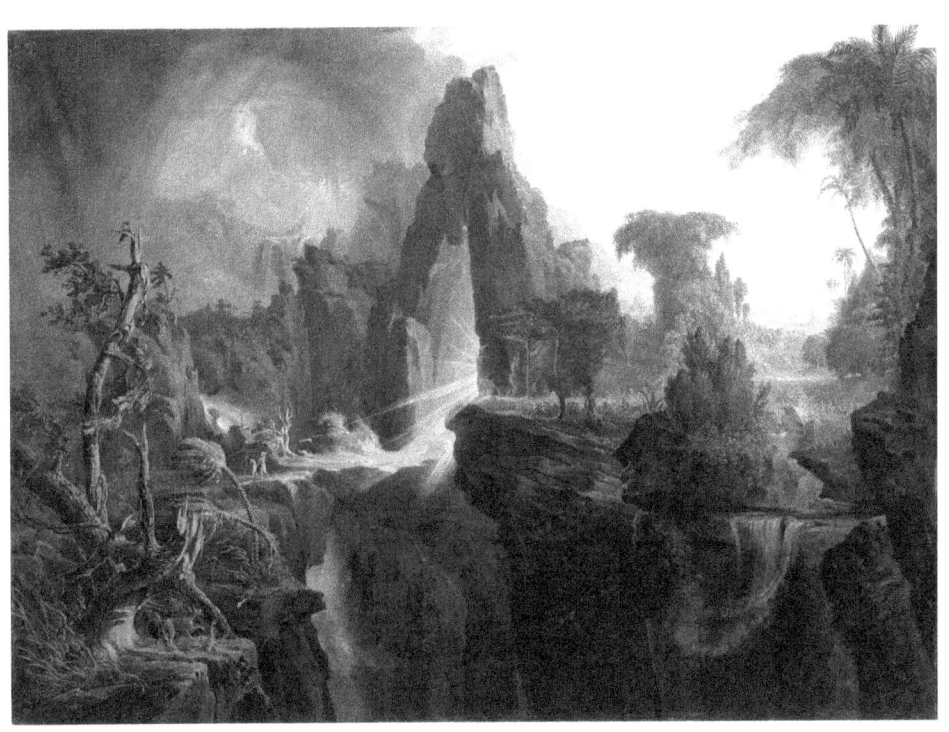

Thomas Cole, Expulsion From the Garden of Eden, 1828,
Museum of Fine Arts, Boston

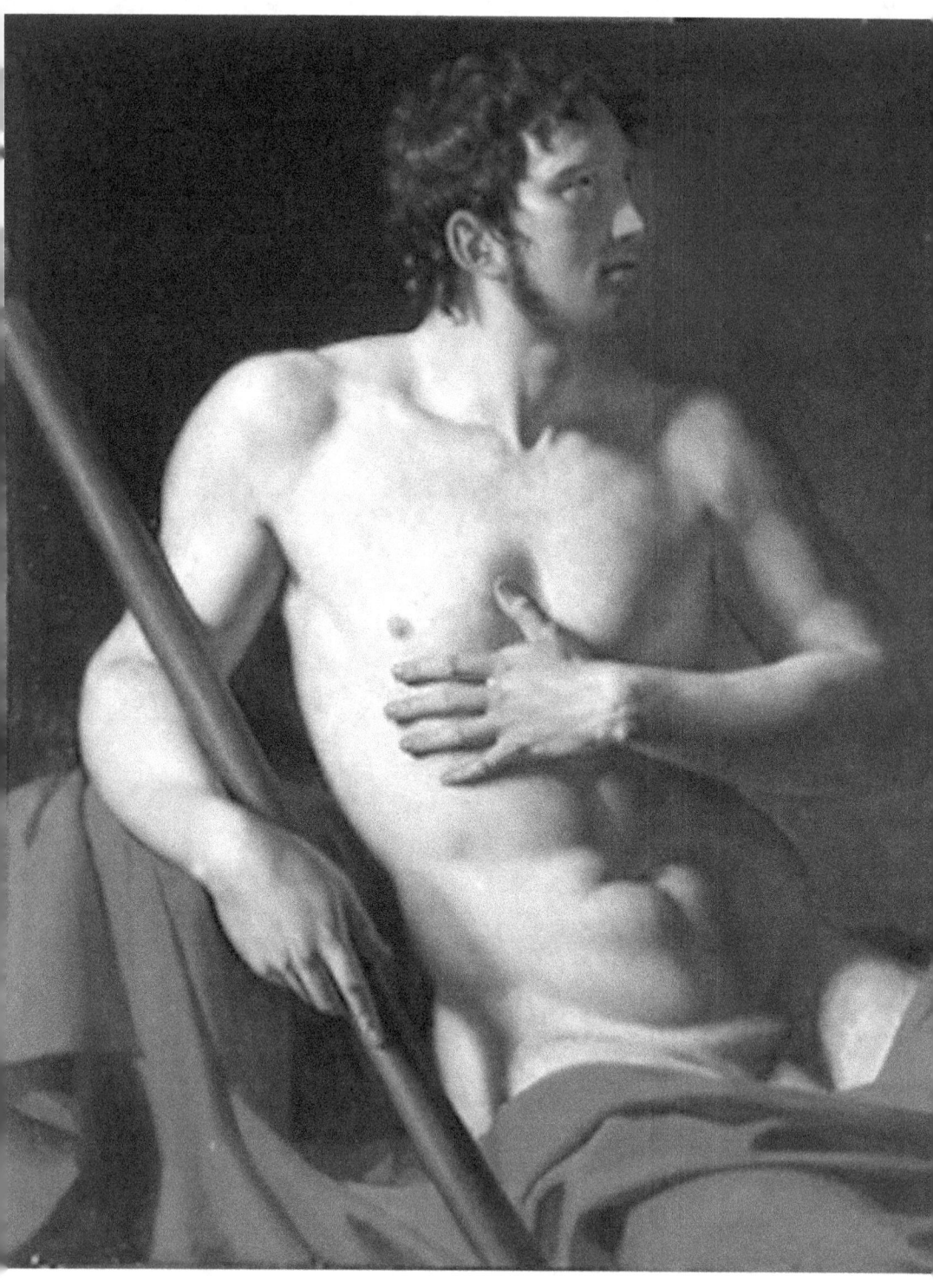

Auguste-Alphonse Gaudar de la Verdine, Male Nude, 1799

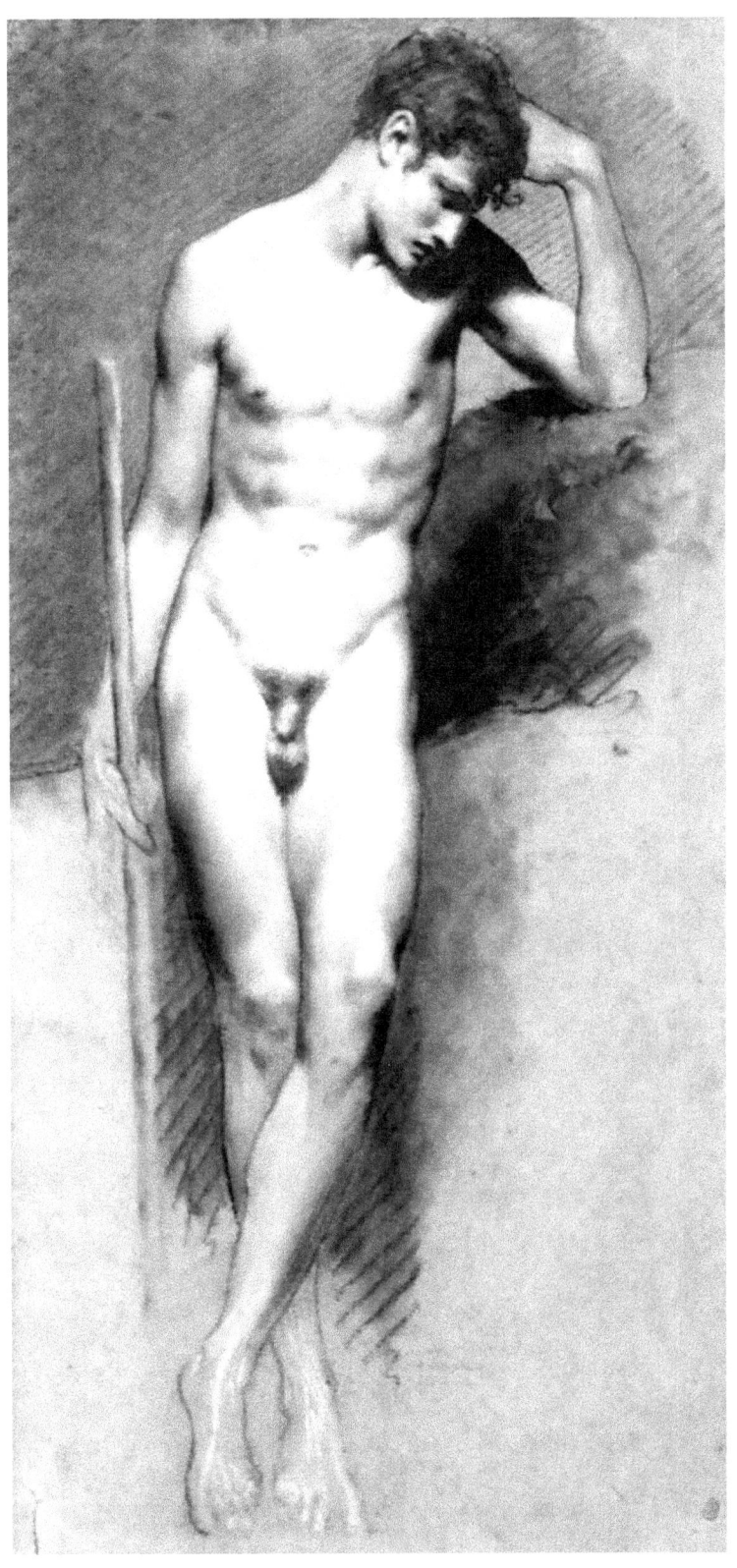

Pierre-Paul Prud'hon (1758-1823), Male Nude Standing

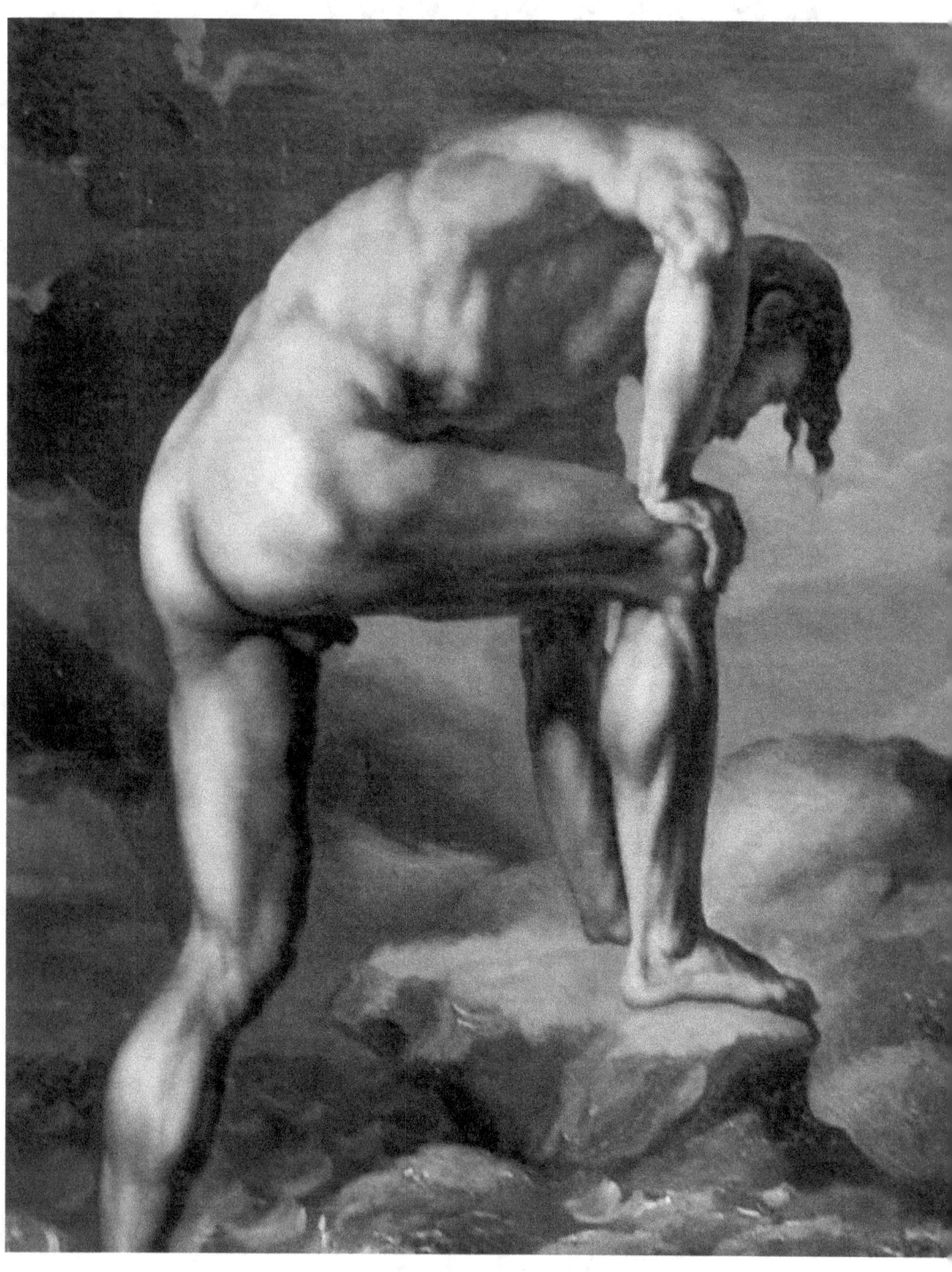

Jean-Louis Andre Theodore Géricault, A Shipwreck, c. 1819

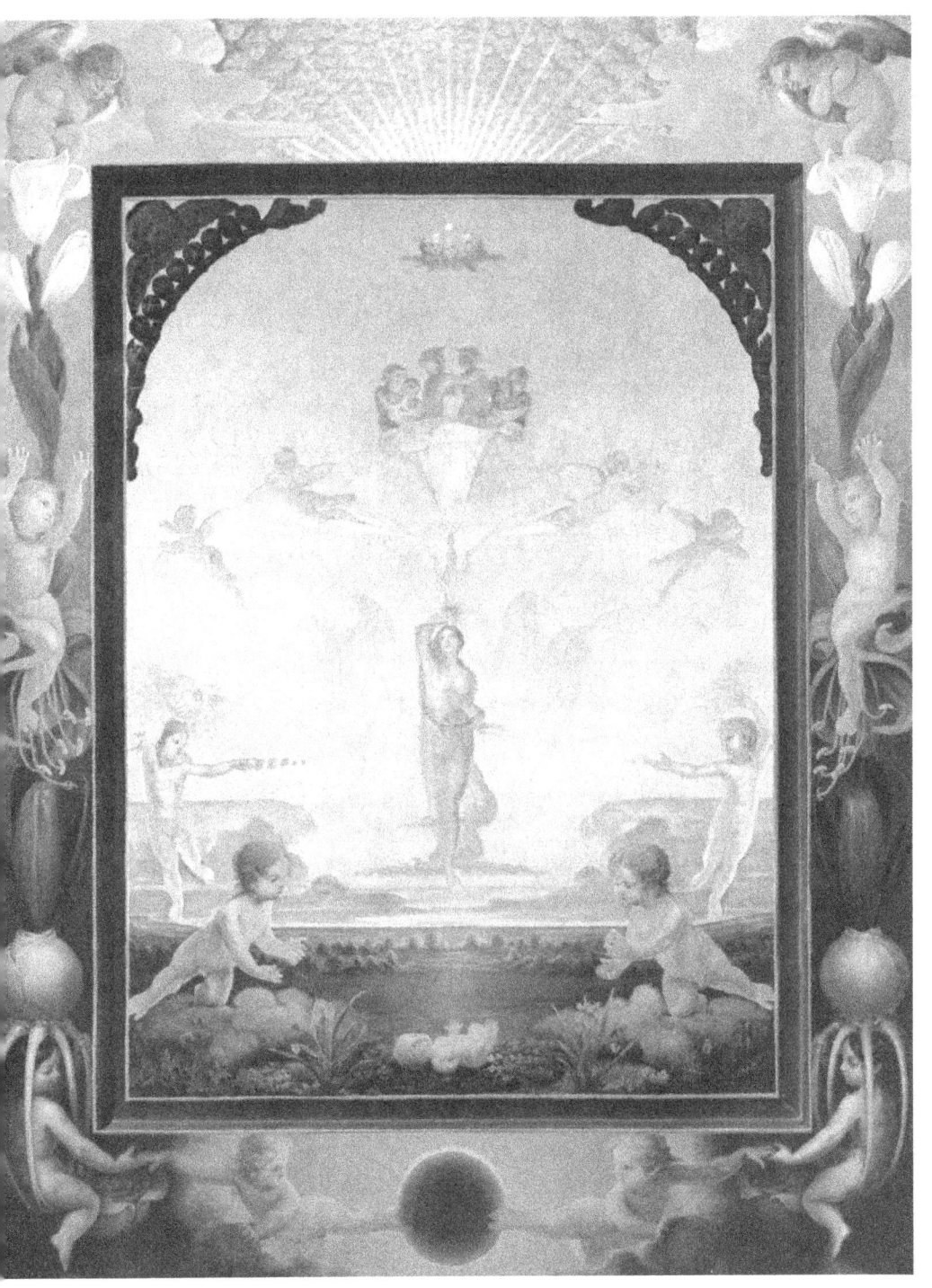

Philipp Otto Runge, Morning, 1808, Hamburg

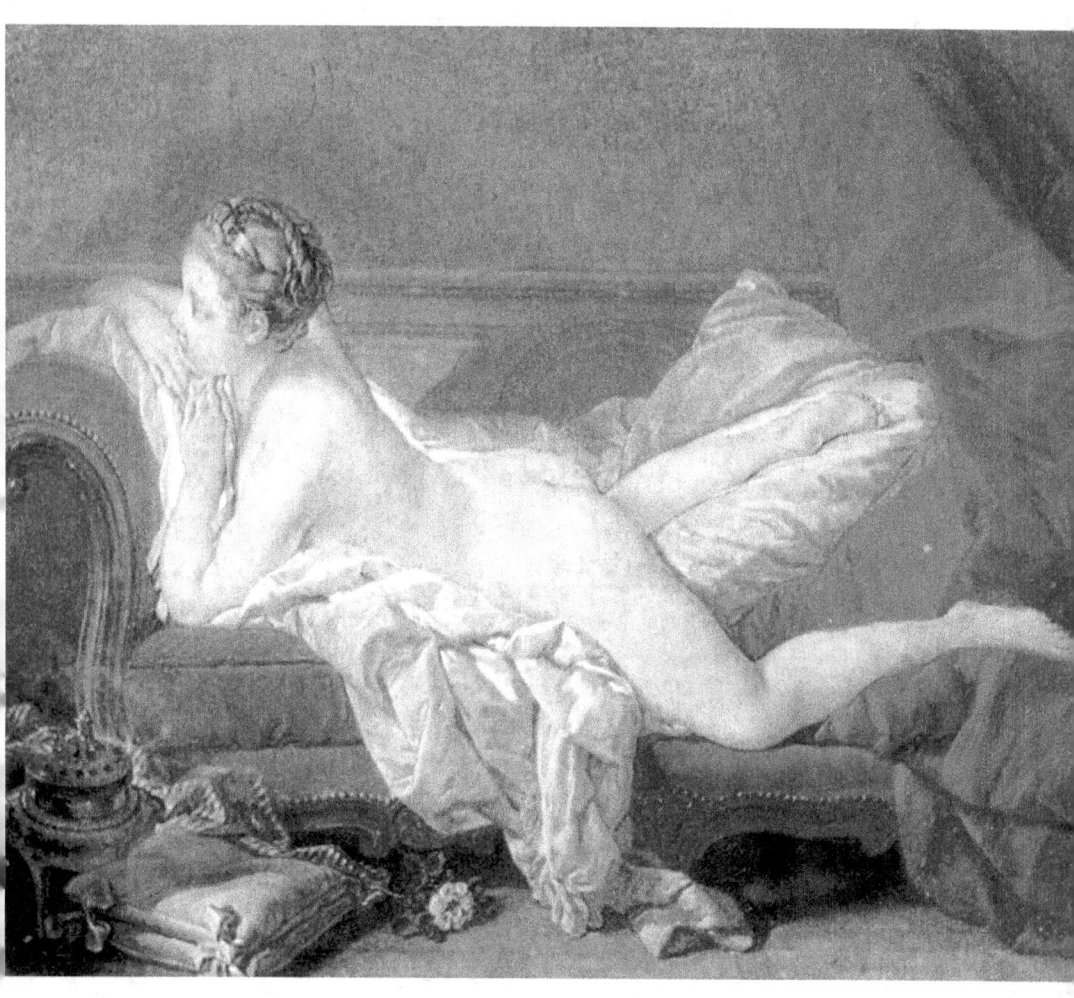

François Boucher, Madamoiselle O'Murphy, 1751

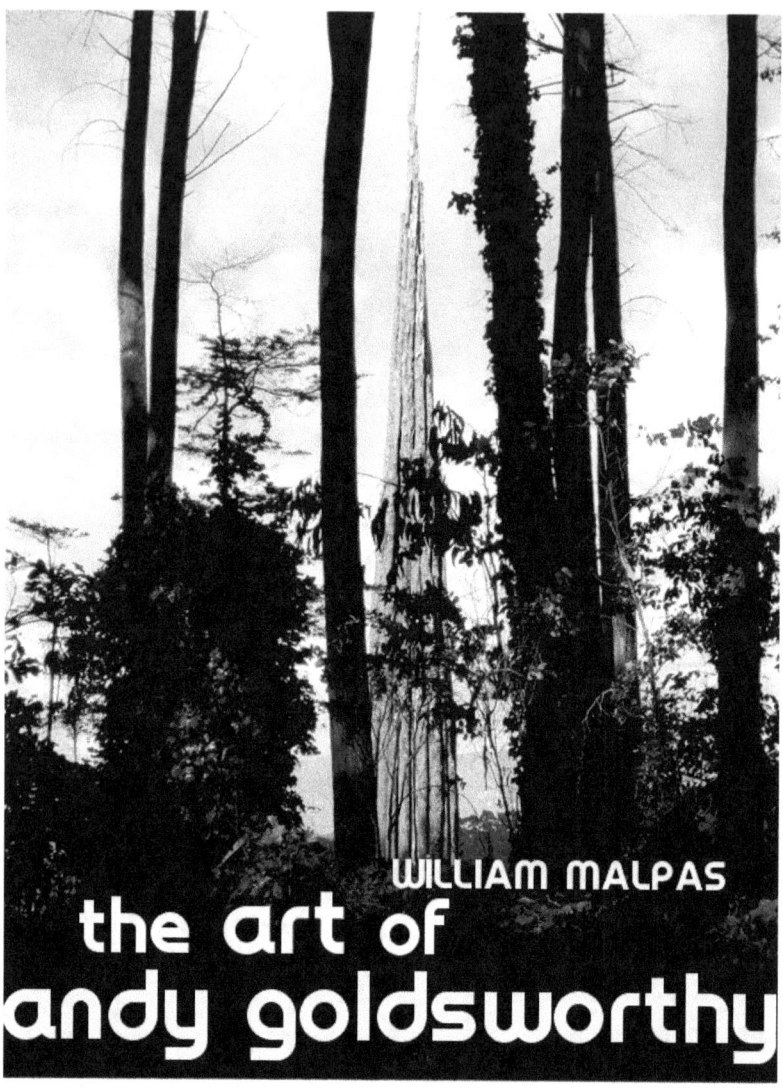

WILLIAM MALPAS
the art of
andy goldsworthy

This is the most comprehensive and detailed account of the art of Andy Goldsworthy available.

This study of Andy Goldsworthy discusses all of Goldsworthy's major exhibitions, books and projects, including the *Sheepfolds* project; *Garden of Stones* in New York; TV and dance collaborations; and the books *Wood, Stone, Time* and *Passage*. William Malpas surveys all of Goldsworthy's output, and analyzes his relation with other land artists such as Robert Smithson, the Christos, Walter de Maria, Chris Drury, Richard Long and David Nash; women sculptors; sculpture in the modern era; and Goldsworthy's place in the contemporary British art scene.

The book has been updated and revised for this new edition.

ISBN 9781861714107 Pbk   ISBN 9781861714114 Hbk
Fully illustrated   www.crmoon.com

MAURICE SENDAK

& the art of children's book illustration

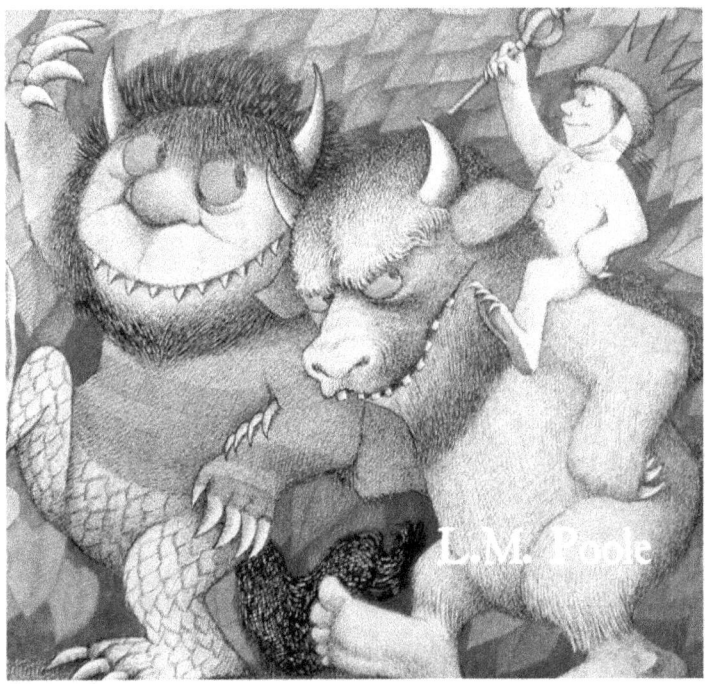

Maurice Sendak is the widely acclaimed American children's book author and illustrator. This critical study focuses on his famous trilogy, *Where the Wild Things Are*, *In the Night Kitchen* and *Outside Over There*, as well as the early works and Sendak's superb depictions of the Grimm Brothers' fairy tales in *The Juniper Tree*. L.M. Poole begins with a chapter on children's book illustration, in particular the treatment of fairy tales. Sendak's work is situated within the history of children's book illustration, and he is compared with many contemporary authors.

Fully illustrated. The book has been revised and updated for this edition.
ISBN 9781861714282 Pbk   ISBN 9781861713469 Hbk

Beauties, Beasts, and Enchantment

CLASSIC FRENCH FAIRY TALES

Translated and with an Introduction
by Jack Zipes

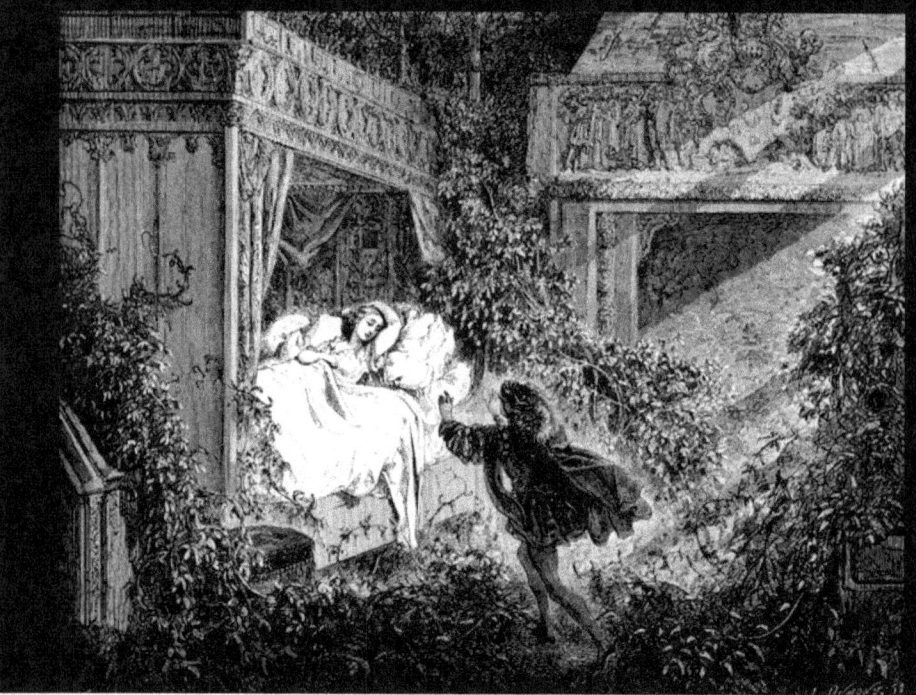

A collection of 36 classic French fairy tales translated by renowned writer Jack Zipes.
Cinderella, Beauty and the Beast, Sleeping Beauty and *Little Red Riding Hood* are among the
classic fairy tales in this amazing book.
Includes illustrations from fairy tale collections.
Jack Zipes has written and published widely on fairy tales.

'Terrific... a succulent array of 17th and 18th century 'salon' fairy tales'
- *The New York Times Book Review*

'These tales are adventurous, thrilling in a way fairy tales are meant to be... The translation
from the French is modern, happily free of archaic and hyperbolic language... a fine and
sophisticated collection' - *New York Tribune*

'Enjoyable to read... a unique collection of French regional folklore' - *Library Journal*

'Charming stories accompanied by attractive pen-and-ink drawings' - *Chattanooga Times*

Introduction and illustrations 612pp.   ISBN 9781861712510 Pbk   ISBN 9781861713193 Hbk

CRESCENT MOON PUBLISHING

web: www.crmoon.com e-mail: cresmopub@yahoo.co.uk

ARTS, PAINTING, SCULPTURE

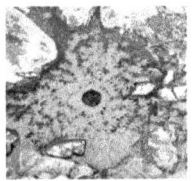

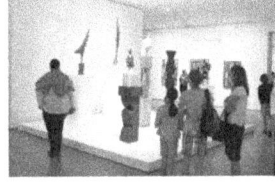

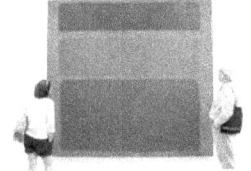

The Art of Andy Goldsworthy
Andy Goldsworthy: Touching Nature
Andy Goldsworthy in Close-Up
Andy Goldsworthy: Pocket Guide
Andy Goldsworthy In America
Land Art: A Complete Guide
The Art of Richard Long
Richard Long: Pocket Guide
Land Art In the UK
Land Art in Close-Up
Land Art In the U.S.A.
Land Art: Pocket Guide
Installation Art in Close-Up
Minimal Art and Artists In the 1960s and After
Colourfield Painting
Land Art DVD, TV documentary
Andy Goldsworthy DVD, TV documentary
The Erotic Object: Sexuality in Sculpture From Prehistory to the Present Day
Sex in Art: Pornography and Pleasure in Painting and Sculpture
Postwar Art
Sacred Gardens: The Garden in Myth, Religion and Art
Glorification: Religious Abstraction in Renaissance and 20th Century Art
Early Netherlandish Painting
Leonardo da Vinci
Piero della Francesca
Giovanni Bellini
Fra Angelico: Art and Religion in the Renaissance
Mark Rothko: The Art of Transcendence
Frank Stella: American Abstract Artist
Jasper Johns
Brice Marden
Alison Wilding: The Embrace of Sculpture
Vincent van Gogh: Visionary Landscapes
Eric Gill: Nuptials of God
Constantin Brancusi: Sculpting the Essence of Things
Max Beckmann
Caravaggio
Gustave Moreau
Egon Schiele: Sex and Death In Purple Stockings
Delizioso Fotografico Fervore: Works In Process 1
Sacro Cuore: Works In Process 2
The Light Eternal: J.M.W. Turner
The Madonna Glorified: Karen Arthurs

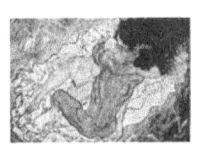

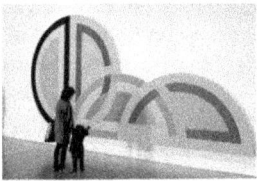

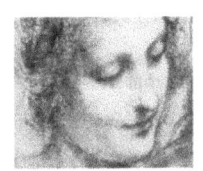

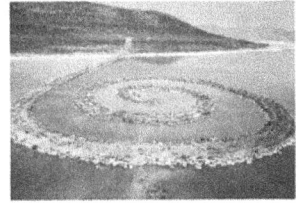

LITERATURE

J.R.R. Tolkien: The Books, The Films, The Whole Cultural Phenomenon
J.R.R. Tolkien: Pocket Guide
Tolkien's Heroic Quest
The *Earthsea* Books of Ursula Le Guin
Beauties, Beasts and Enchantment: Classic French Fairy Tales
German Popular Stories by the Brothers Grimm
Philip Pullman and *His Dark Materials*
Sexing Hardy: Thomas Hardy and Feminism
Thomas Hardy's *Tess of the d'Urbervilles*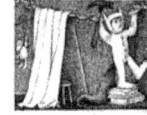
Thomas Hardy's *Jude the Obscure*
Thomas Hardy: The Tragic Novels
Love and Tragedy: Thomas Hardy
The Poetry of Landscape in Hardy
Wessex Revisited: Thomas Hardy and John Cowper Powys
Wolfgang Iser: Essays and Interviews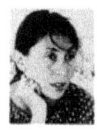
Petrarch, Dante and the Troubadours
Maurice Sendak and the Art of Children's Book Illustration
Andrea Dworkin
Cixous, Irigaray, Kristeva: The *Jouissance* of French Feminism
Julia Kristeva: Art, Love, Melancholy, Philosophy, Semiotics and Psychoanalysis
Hélène Cixous I Love You: The *Jouissance* of Writing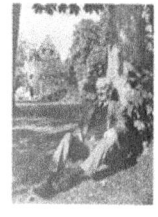
Luce Irigaray: Lips, Kissing, and the Politics of Sexual Difference
Peter Redgrove: Here Comes the Flood
Peter Redgrove: Sex-Magic-Poetry-Cornwall
Lawrence Durrell: Between Love and Death, East and West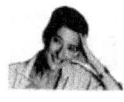
Love, Culture & Poetry: Lawrence Durrell
Cavafy: Anatomy of a Soul
German Romantic Poetry: Goethe, Novalis, Heine, Hölderlin
Feminism and Shakespeare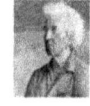
Shakespeare: Love, Poetry & Magic
The Passion of D.H. Lawrence
D.H. Lawrence: Symbolic Landscapes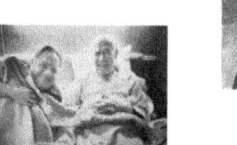
D.H. Lawrence: Infinite Sensual Violence
Rimbaud: Arthur Rimbaud and the Magic of Poetry
The Ecstasies of John Cowper Powys
Sensualism and Mythology: The Wessex Novels of John Cowper Powys
Amorous Life: John Cowper Powys and the Manifestation of Affectivity (H.W. Fawkner)
Postmodern Powys: New Essays on John Cowper Powys (Joe Boulter)
Rethinking Powys: Critical Essays on John Cowper Powys
Paul Bowles & Bernardo Bertolucci
Rainer Maria Rilke
Joseph Conrad: *Heart of Darkness*
In the Dim Void: Samuel Beckett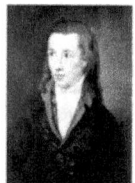
Samuel Beckett Goes into the Silence
André Gide: Fiction and Fervour
Jackie Collins and the Blockbuster Novel
Blinded By Her Light: The Love-Poetry of Robert Graves
The Passion of Colours: Travels In Mediterranean Lands
Poetic Forms

POETRY

Ursula Le Guin: Walking In Cornwall
Peter Redgrove: Here Comes The Flood
Peter Redgrove: Sex-Magic-Poetry-Cornwall
Dante: Selections From the Vita Nuova
Petrarch, Dante and the Troubadours
William Shakespeare: Sonnets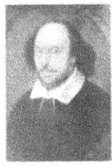
William Shakespeare: Complete Poems
Blinded By Her Light: The Love-Poetry of Robert Graves
Emily Dickinson: Selected Poems
Emily Brontë: Poems
Thomas Hardy: Selected Poems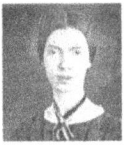
Percy Bysshe Shelley: Poems
John Keats: Selected Poems
Joh n Keats: Poems of 1820
D.H. Lawrence: Selected Poems
Edmund Spenser: Poems
Edmund Spenser: Amoretti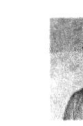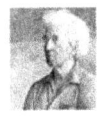
John Donne: Poems
Henry Vaughan: Poems
Sir Thomas Wyatt: Poems
Robert Herrick: Selected Poems
Rilke: Space, Essence and Angels in the Poetry of Rainer Maria Rilke
Rainer Maria Rilke: Selected Poems
Friedrich Hölderlin: Selected Poems
Arseny Tarkovsky: Selected Poems
Arthur Rimbaud: Selected Poems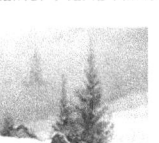
Arthur Rimbaud: A Season in Hell
Arthur Rimbaud and the Magic of Poetry
Novalis: Hymns To the Night
German Romantic Poetry
Paul Verlaine: Selected Poems
Elizaethan Sonnet Cycles
D.J. Enright: By-Blows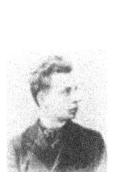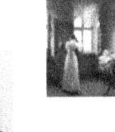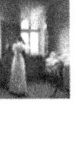
Jeremy Reed: Brigitte's Blue Heart
Jeremy Reed: Claudia Schiffer's Red Shoes
Gorgeous Little Orpheus
Radiance: New Poems
Crescent Moon Book of Nature Poetry
Crescent Moon Book of Love Poetry
Crescent Moon Book of Mystical Poetry
Crescent Moon Book of Elizabethan Love Poetry
Crescent Moon Book of Metaphysical Poetry
Crescent Moon Book of Romantic Poetry
Pagan America: New American Poetry

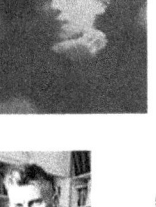
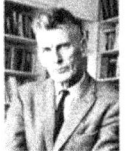
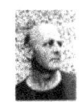
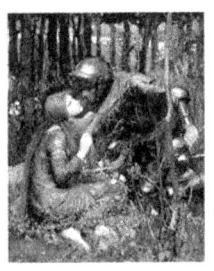
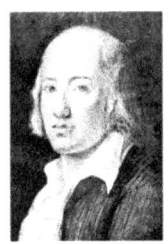
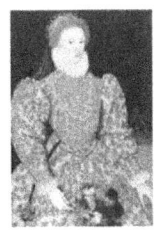

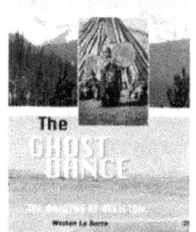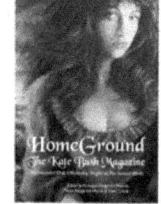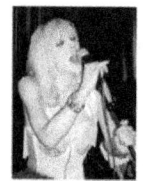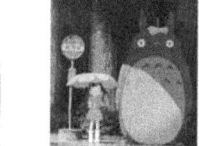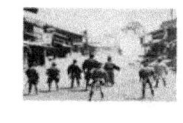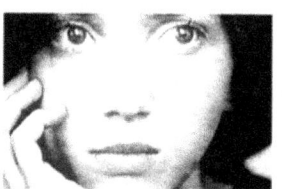

www.ingramcontent.com/pod-product-compliance
Lightning Source LLC
Chambersburg PA
CBHW051325220526
45468CB00004B/1502